C# Programming Interview Questions, Answers and Explanations: Programming C# Certification Review

By Terry Sanchez- Clark

C# Programming Interview Questions, Answers and
Explanations: Programming C# Certification Review

1-933804-55-6

Edited by: Jamie Fisher

Please visit our website at www.itcookbook.com

Table of Contents

C# Programming Interview Questions, Answers and Explanations: Programming C# Certification Review

By Terry Sanchez- Clark

Question 1: Retrieve items from the array list of class

I have the following class:

```
public class myclass
  {
  private int RoomNumber;
  private string User;

  public myclass()
    {
    RoomNumber = -1;
    User = "";
    }
    myclass(int roomnum, string user)
    {
    RoomNumber = roomnum;
    User = user;
    }
    public int myRoomNumber
    {
    get { return RoomNumber; }
    set { RoomNumber = value; }
    }
    public string myUser
    {
    get { return User; }
    set { User = value; }
    }

  }
```

Here is how I created an array list of this class objects:

```
myclass croom = new myclass();
private ArrayList roomArrayList = new ArrayList();

public void addrooms(int RoomNumber, string user)
  {
  this.invitations.myRoomNumber = RoomNumber;
  this.invitations.myUser = user;
```

```
   this.roomArrayList.Add(croom);
   }
```

The above code works fine, but the method below doesn't work. I don't get
the correct values in my array. In this method I am trying to
retrieve the information from the array list, and I am trying to
get the list of all rooms a particular user is in.

```
public int[] GetRooms(string user)
   {
   int roomnum;
   int[] userlistarray = new string[MaxNum];
   int i = 0;

   foreach (myclass item in roomArrayList)
   {
   if ( item.myUser==user)

   {
   roomnum = item.myRoomNumber;
   userlistarray[i] = roomnum;
   i++;
   }
   else
   {
   userlistarray=null;
   }

   }
   return userlistarray;
   }
```

What is the correct syntax ?

A: Assuming this is how you populated the 'myclass' collection:

```
myclass croom = new myclass();
private ArrayList roomArrayList = new ArrayList();

public void addrooms(int RoomNumber, string user)
   {
   // You set a new room to <invitations>, but...
   this.invitations.myRoomNumber = RoomNumber;
```

```
this.invitations.myUser = user;

// you're adding croom to this.roomArrayList?
this.roomArrayList.Add(croom);
}
```

This code will populate items for "roomArrayList", but all points to the single instance of croom.

Check if you're adding the correct 'myclass' instance to "this.roomArrayList"?

You need to make new 'myclass' objects every call of "addrooms()" to avoid collecting references of the same object, rather than unique copies=.

```
public void addrooms(int RoomNumber, string user)
{
// ... lines omitted for brevity
// add a new myclass
this.roomArrayList.Add(new myclass(RoomNumber, user));
}
```

Question 2: Start a 'GUI app' from a service in 'Remote Desktop'

I can start any program (with a GUI) from a service. This works great on W2003 when you are logged in (physically) on the machine. However, when connecting from 'Remote Desktop'{XE "'Remote Desktop'"}, it seems that the process starts on another desktop or session.

Is it possible to start the process on the active (remote desktop) session from the service?

A: Services should not run any code that interacts directly with the desktop. Yes, it will occasionally work. But what's happening is you're getting lucky because some internal values just happen to line up.

The desktop (Window Station, more correctly) doesn't get created until the user logs in, and services start when Windows boots. So, if a user never logs in, there will never be a desktop created, and nothing for the service to interact with.

If you do need to interact with a desktop, do like 'SQL Server' does and split the engine apart from the UI. The engine runs as a service (meaning it starts when Windows starts), and the UI (the service monitor that sits in the clock tray) runs when the user logs in.

Question 3: Use PIA without installing 'Office'

I have an app that uses the 'Excel Interop Class'{XE "'Excel Interop Class'"} to open a worksheet (not workbook) to modify the header and import the data into a database. The worksheet is downloaded from a third party web app.

It works fine for development because my box has Office 2003 installed. However, when I transfer the files to the testing server I get assembly errors stating that the Excel PIA has broken references.

I tried coping over the 'excel.exe' file that is directly refaced. I placed the file in the 'bin' and "C:\Program File\Microsoft Office\OFFICE11"directory, but the assembly is still missing references. The data doesn't start until row 24, before that was an explanation on how the file was created. I used the interop to remove those rows, and then select from excel using 'OleDb'.

Is it possible to install just the PIA and COM objects without installing the entire office suite on the server?

Does installing Office/PIA's require additional licensing?

A: If you intend to use a component part of Excel, the machine on which it runs should be licensed for it. You could use the "System.Data.OleDb" namespace to pull data from an Excel workbook without requiring interop. This would get around the licensing issue. Using 'OleDb' will remove all interop worries and Excel dependencies.

Take note that using "IV65536" as the 'end cell reference' will not result in thousands of empty rows, only rows with data will be returned. You can ignore the first 24 rows by using the following:

```
using (System.Data.OleDb.OleDbConnection c = new
System.Data.OleDb.OleDbConnection("Provider=Microsoft.Jet.OLED
B.4.0;Data Source=C:\\Test.xls;Extended Properties=\"Excel 8.0;\""))
{
    System.Data.OleDb.OleDbDataAdapter da = new
System.Data.OleDb.OleDbDataAdapter("SELECT * FROM
```

```
[Sheet1$A24:IV65536]", c);

   DataTable dt = new DataTable();

   da.Fill(dt);

   dataGrid1.DataSource = dt;
}
```

Question 4: Converting "DateTime" to numeric

Is there a ".net" function that will take a 'datetime' value?

Ex: "5/5/2006 12:00:00" and output it in this format: 05052006120000.

A: You can use the following:

```
System.DateTime.Now.ToString ("MMddyyyyhhmmss")
```

Question 5: Data Grid and Multiple Data Sets

I can view data with the data grid like everyone else, but what I'm trying to do is loop through a list box of server names and fill just one data grid with the results from each server.

For example:

The server will be each server in the list box.

Strings connect = "Server=" + server + ";DataBase=msdb;Integrated Security=SSPI";

select * from SYSTABLE

Now, as I run through the list box of servers I will retrieve different results in which I would like to place in 1 data grid. All column names are the same.

SERVER	COLUMN1	COLUMN2	COLUMN3
SQL1	Bob Smith	Oakwood	Florida
SQL2	Brian Kite	Oakland	Georgia
SQL3	Frank Sinatra	Spider	Ohio

How would I go about doing this, this is what I'm working on so far?

rsadapter.Fill(sqldataset, rsconnect);

dataGrid1.DataSource = sqldataset.Tables[rsconnect];

dataTable = sqldataset.Tables[dataTable] + sqldataset.Tables[a];
(This part is not working.)

I am trying to add data to the data table.

How can I resolve this problem?

A: You could just make a "Data Table". Fill the data table with the data that you want, and then just make the data table the source for the data grid. The data table has much less overhead.

```
// you have a set number of columns
// create a datatable and define them
DataTable dt = new DataTable("stathread");

dt.Columns.Add("SERVER");
dt.Columns.Add("COLUMN1");
dt.Columns.Add("COLUMN2");
dt.Columns.Add("COLUMN3");

// get your server data out of the list box
// DO SOME STUFF HERE

// make a loop that cycles through the list of returned servers
for (int i = 0; i < returned_server_count; i++)
{
    // define the array that will hold the values for each row
    string[] theRow = new string[4];

    // get the server name from your listbox at position i,
    // assign it to the first item in the array
    theRow[0] = "your retrieved server name";

    // do your stuff to get the dynamic data
    // based on the value you retrieved above
    // assign it to the other array positions
    theRow[1] = "Stuff you got for col 1";
    theRow[2] = "Stuff you got for col 2";
    theRow[3] = "Stuff you got for col 3";

    // make a row based on the datatable schema
    DataRow dr = dt.NewRow();

    // assign the array to the row
    dr.ItemArray = theRow;

    // add the row to the table
    dt.Rows.Add(dr);
}

// set the datasource
dataGrid1.DataSource = dt;
```

There is another suggestion you can use a "SqlCommand", "SqlConnection", and then a "SqlDataReader".

You can also take a different approach by cloning and copying the data to a new data table, and then view it.

Question 6:
"GetManifestResourceStream"

What is the meaning of "GetManifestResourceStream"?

A: It allows you to pull resources (Images, Icons, etc) which are included in your solution.

So if you have

```
My Solution
  References
  Images
    -FastForward.gif  (Embedded Resource)
  AssemblyInfo.cs
  Form1.cs
```

your form could say:

```
Stream s =
Assembly.GetExecutingAssembly().GetManifestResourceStream("My
Solution.Images.FastForward.gif");

PictureBox1.Image = Image.FromStream(s);
```

Now, your picture has been pulled from the embedded solution resource file{ XE "embedded solution resource file" } and is being used in your picture box. Remember that any resource that you want to use this way must have the 'Compile Action' property set to "Embedded Resource".

Question 7: Hotkeys

How can I block the hot keys of excel, word or another program like this?

Is it possible if I open these kinds of files from C#?

A: You can install a 'system-wide' keyboard hook. You can check which app has the focus and if it's the one you're interested in, and then remove the keystroke from the queue.

Question 8: COM interop

How can I use COM interop in C#?

I am working on an application that uses BITS feature in windows.

Is there a link for that?

A: You can just add a reference to the COM DLL{XE "COM DLL"} on your project by going through "Project/Add Reference, COM tab". After adding, you'll find on the Solution Explorer that an "*.Interop.Dll" was created.

The interop DLL is a '.NET' assembly, and is used like how you use the "System.dll assembly of .NET" with all the '.NET' classes and enums. It's basically a '.NET' wrapper that does the marshalling of data as you consume the COM objects.

What you will really need is a good documentation on BITS. But if you still need an in-depth material about interops, just google "COM interop .net".

Question 9: SQL issues

I have the following example dataset:

```
pubdateid  reelid  Icount
1--------- 1-------1
1--------- 2-------2
1--------- 3-------3
1--------- 4-------4
2--------- 1-------4
2--------- 2-------3
2--------- 3-------2
2--------- 4-------1
3--------- 1-------1
3--------- 2-------1
3--------- 3-------2
3--------- 4-------2
```

From this, I need to fetch the highlighted rows. I need each "pubdateid" row that has the lowest amount in count. If the count has more than one, that is the lowest. But the same as another, I need to take the record with the highest 'reelid'.

So far I have come up with this (minus the equal count part):

declare @tempstr varchar(8000)
declare @pubdateIDs varchar(3000)

set @pubdateIDs = '8347151, 4, 7608501'

set @tempstr = 'select pubdateid, reelid, min(Icount) from #MR_temp where pubdateid in (' + @pubdateids + ') group by pubdateid, reelid'
exec (@tempstr)

I assumed it will give me a list of all the "pubdatids" with the lowest count, but instead it just returns the entire table.

How can I correct this?

A: You can use the following code in your SQL:

```
Select
  pubdateid,
  max(reelid),
  iCount
from #MR_temp t 1
where pubdateid in (@pubdateids) <----set this correctly in your code
  and iCount = (select min(t2.icount)
         from #MR_temp t2
         where t2.pubdateid = t1.pubdateid)
group by pubdateid, iCount
```

Question 10: Finding out what a statement is doing

I have this statement that doesn't give me the results I expected:

```
if (
                (
                i != mnPosition
                )
                &&
                (
                    (
                        (
                        Convert.ToInt32(img.ImageData.Tables[0].Rows[i]
["imageid"]) ==
Convert.ToInt32(img.ImageData.Tables[0].Rows[i]["parentid"])
                        )
                        &&
                        (
                        Convert.ToInt32(img.ImageData.Tables[0].Rows[i]
["imageid"]) - Convert.ToInt32(img.ImageData.Tables[0].Rows[i -
1]["parentid"]) > 1
                        )
                    )
                    ||
                    (
                        (
                        Convert.ToInt32(img.ImageData.Tables[0].Rows[i]
["imageid"]) !=
Convert.ToInt32(img.ImageData.Tables[0].Rows[i]["parentid"])
                        &&
                        img.ImageData.Tables[0].Rows[i]["parentid"] !=
null
                        )
                        &&
                        (
                        Convert.ToInt32(img.ImageData.Tables[0].Rows[i]
["parentid"]) - Convert.ToInt32(img.ImageData.Tables[0].Rows[i -
1]["parentid"]) >= 1
                        )
                    )
                    ||
```

```
                        (
                                img.ImageData.Tables[0].Rows[i]["parentid"] ==
null

                                &&
                                img.ImageData.Tables[0].Rows[i-1]["parentid"] !=
null

                                &&
                                (
                                        Convert.ToInt32(img.ImageData.Tables[0].Row
s[i]["imageid"]) - Convert.ToInt32(img.ImageData.Tables[0].Rows[i -
1]["parentid"]) > 1
                                )
                        )
                        ||
                        (
                                img.ImageData.Tables[0].Rows[i]["parentid"] ==
null

                                &&
                                img.ImageData.Tables[0].Rows[i-1]["parentid"] ==
null

                                &&
                                (
                                        Convert.ToInt32(img.ImageData.Tables[0].Row
s[i]["imageid"]) - Convert.ToInt32(img.ImageData.Tables[0].Rows[i -
1]["imageid"]) > 1
                                )
                        )
                )
        )
```

Is there a way for me to throw message box into the statement, or some other way for me to find out exactly what is happening?

A: Break each of the "pieces" of your 'if statement' down and use them to test the values of some of the 'Boolean variables'. It can be something like this:

```
bool step1 =
((Convert.ToInt32(img.ImageData.Tables[0].Rows[i]["imageid"]) ==
Convert.ToInt32(img.ImageData.Tables[0].Rows[i]["parentid"]))
 &&
(Convert.ToInt32(img.ImageData.Tables[0].Rows[i]["imageid"]) -
Convert.ToInt32(img.ImageData.Tables[0].Rows[i - 1]["parentid"]) >
1));
```

```
bool step2 =
((Convert.ToInt32(img.ImageData.Tables[0].Rows[i]["imageid"]) !=
Convert.ToInt32(img.ImageData.Tables[0].Rows[i]["parentid"]))
 &&
(img.ImageData.Tables[0].Rows[i]["parentid"] != null)
 &&
(Convert.ToInt32(img.ImageData.Tables[0].Rows[i]["parentid"]) -
Convert.ToInt32(img.ImageData.Tables[0].Rows[i - 1]["parentid"]) >=
1);

bool step3 = ...

if ((i != mnPosition) && (step1 || step2 || step3))
```

This way, you'll be able to check the value of each condition along the way. You can break it down even further if you need to.

Question 11: tsql temp table

I have the following SQL:

```
declare @tempstr varchar(8000)
declare @freds varchar(3000)

set @freds = '8347151, 4, 7608501'

set @tempstr = 'create table temp as select fredid, bubbid, count(dotid)
from freds where fredid in (' + @freds + ')'

exec (@tempstr)
```

But I am receiving this error:

```
Server: Msg 156, Level 15, State 1, Line 1
Incorrect syntax near the keyword 'as'.
```

It hovers over "declare @tempstr varchar(8000)" when I click on the error message.

Can I build a temp table in tsql?

If so, how do I do it?

A: You must put the symbol "#"in front of all temporary tables.

Try this:

```
declare @tempstr varchar(8000)
declare @freds varchar(3000)

set @freds = '8347151, 4, 7608501'

set @tempstr = 'select fredid, bubbid, count(dotid) into #temp from
freds where fredid in (' + @freds + ')'

exec (@tempstr)
```

Or you can try the following:

```
declare @tempstr varchar(8000)
declare @freds varchar(3000)

Create table #temp
(
fredid int,
bubbid int,
numRecs int
)

set @freds = '8347151, 4, 7608501'

set @tempstr = 'Insert into #temp(fredid, bubbid, numRecs)select
fredid, bubbid, count(dotid) from freds where fredid in (' + @freds + ')'

exec (@tempstr)
```

Question 12: Syntax

I'm currently beginning a project using IBM MQ for '.net', but one line of syntax made me a little confused.

How can I convert the following to 'vb.net'?

Code:

```
int openOptions = MQC.MQOO_INPUT_AS_Q_DEF |
MQC.MQOO_OUTPUT ;
```

I don't know what the "pipe" translates to.

A: The pipe is an "Or" operator (that's what I thought, but for some reason I thought an "or" was two pipes). It's a 'bitwise-OR', versus the two-pipe version which is a 'logical-OR'.

So, 2 | 1 returns 3 because the bit-patterns are:

```
00000010
00000001
=========
00000011
```

You can also check out the following site for more explanation:

http://en.wikipedia.org/wiki/Bitwise_operation

Question 13: Import a "*.reg" file

How can I import a "*.reg" file in C#?
In 'VbScript', I would use "WshShell.Run" ("regedit.exe /s f.reg").

A: You can try the following code:

```
System.Diagnostics.Process.Start("regedit.exe /s f.reg");
```

Question 14: Hide a 'Form' when X-button is pressed

I have an application where one of my dialogs was created when the program starts. I like to call "Form.Show()" and "Form.Hide()" to show and hide the form.

When the user presses the 'system-X' button, the form is per default disposed.

How do I prevent that I just want a "Form.Hide()" when the user does that so that I can call "Form.Show()" again without making a new instance of it?

A: In the closing event of the form/dialog, try the following code:

```
e.cancel = true;
this.hide();
```

I hope that's all good c#.

You can also try the following:

```
protected override void OnClosing(CancelEventArgs e)
{
e.Cancel = true;
Hide();
//base.OnClosing(e);
}
```

Question 15: XML/SVG SetAttribute Issue xlink:href

I'm working on a code to generate SVG dynamically{XE "generate SVG dynamically"} via the web. When I try to create an element to display one of the shapes in the "def" section of the SVG file, I'm getting unexpected output.

Below, I'm trying to create a node called "use" with the following attribute "xlink:href".

Code:
```
svgElem = SvgXml.CreateElement("use",
"http://www.w3.org/2000/svg");
svgElem.SetAttribute("xlink:href", "#" + sheetName);
RootNode.ChildNodes[1].FirstChild.AppendChild(svgElem);
```

XML Output
Code:
```
<?xml version="1.0" standalone="yes"?>
<svg width="800" height="600"
xmlns="http://www.w3.org/2000/svg">
 <def>
   <rect id="13-81X76.5X3.5" x="0" y="0" widht="800" height="600"
style="fill:none;stroke:rgb(0,0,255);stroke-width:.05" />
 </def>
 <g transform="translate(20, 585)">
  <g transform="scale(0.95, -0.95)">
    <use href="#13-81X76.5X3.5" />
  </g>
 </g>
</svg>
```

Notice that the code is putting out the following:

Code:
```
<use href="#13-81X76.5X3.5" />
```

I expected to see:

Code:
```
<use xlink:href="#13-81X76.5X3.5" />
```

- 25 -

Why is this happening and how can I get the results necessary for the SVG to work properly?

A: You can use the following code:

```
svgElem = SvgXml.CreateElement("use",
"http://www.w3.org/2000/svg");
svgElem.SetAttributeNode("href", "http://www.w3.org/1999/xlink");
svgElem.Attributes["href"].Value = "#" + sheetName;
svgElem.Attributes["href"].Prefix = "xlink";
RootNode.ChildNodes[1].FirstChild.AppendChild(svgElem);
```

Here is the XML:

```
<?xml version="1.0" standalone="yes"?>
<svg width="800" height="600"
xmlns="http://www.w3.org/2000/svg">
  <def>
    <rect id="13-81X76.5X3.5" x="0" y="0" widht="800" height="600"
style="fill:none;stroke:rgb(0,0,255);stroke-width:.05" />
  </def>
  <g transform="translate(20, 585)">
    <g transform="scale(0.95, -0.95)">
      <use xlink:href="#13-81X76.5X3.5"
xmlns:xlink="http://www.w3.org/1999/xlink" />
    </g>
  </g>
</svg>
```

Question 16: Creating decimals with 4 places

I need to have a counter that is an int turn into 4 decimal places. This would be easy enough but each number has to be unique.

So, if I have a counter that is:

1,2,3,4,5,6,7,8,9,10

I need to place it as:

.0001,.0002,.0003,.0004,.0005,.0006,.0007,.0008,.0009,.0010
etc

How can I accomplish this?

A: This can do the trick at a minimum:

Code:

```
for (int i=1; i<11; i++)
{
  System.Double db = i * .0001;
  Console.WriteLine(db.ToString());
}
```

Question 17: Control button

I have the following code:

```
private void BestAvail_Click(object sender, EventArgs e)
{
    MessageBox.Show(e.Equals());
    for (int i = 0; i < mtpPanel.PageCollection.NumPagesSelected; i++)
    {
        mtpPanel.PageCollection[mtpPanel.SelectedPagesArray[i]].BestAvailImage =
!mtpPanel.PageCollection[mtpPanel.SelectedPagesArray[i]].BestAvailImage;
        mtpPanel.PageCollection[mtpPanel.SelectedPagesArray[i]].setBestAvail();
    }
}
```

The problem is I need it to do one of two things. If the button was clicked, I need the above event to run. If the button was clicked with the control button pressed, I need it to do something else.

How do I accomplish this?

A: You can try the following:

add 2 more event handlers - KeyDown and KeyUp

```
private bool controlkeypressed = false;

private void yourcontrol_KeyDown(object sender, KeyEventArgs e)
{
    if (e.KeyCode == Keys.Control)
    {
        controlkeypressed = true;
    }
}

private void yourcontrol_KeyUp(object sender, KeyEventArgs e)
{
    if (e.KeyCode == Keys.Control)
```

```
    {
      controlkeypressed = false;
    }
}

private void BestAvail_Click(object sender, EventArgs e)
    {

    if (controlkeypressed)
    {
       //Do your modified stuff
    }
    else
    {
       //Do your regular stuff
    }
}
```

Another suggestion is to try the following:

this.mtbpPanel.KeyUp += new EventHandler(control_KeyUp); //used with best available to find out whether the [ctrl] button is pressed during the click
this.mtbpPanel.KeyDown += new EventHandler(control_KeyDown); // same as above

To build the event handler, try the following:

C:\Main.cs(614): Method 'QC.QCMain.control_KeyUp(object, System.Windows.Forms.KeyEventArgs)' does not match delegate 'void System.EventHandler(object, System.EventArgs

this.mtbpPanel.KeyUp += new KeyEventHandler(control_KeyUp);

Your control has to have focus, so you may have to click on the panel before it will register the event. The other option is to put the event handler on the form and set the "KeyPreview" property to "True".

Question 18: Previewing images (64*64) control

I like to preview some image objects in "64*64" format in some kind of control.

Is there any ".NET" control for that?

I only found the "ListView" control, but with that I can only preview pictures in "16*16" format. That is not enough for me.

How can I improve it?

A: You can use the "PictureBox" control and add it to a panel.

Also, when you get the 'Image', I recommend getting only the 'thumb nail' from the image.

> Image.GetThumbnail(); (or something similar)

Question 19: "Treeview" node

I created a lazy loading treeview. The tree only has 2 levels. I allow loading the first level. The second is loaded only if the user expands it. To make the 'plus' appear for nodes that contains 'children', I add one node with an empty string under each first level node. The onlycode that deals with expanding and collapsing a node is in the "MouseDown" event. Sometimes, the node won't collapse but it would clear the 'child' nodes and add one blank text node.

Code:

```
private void phoneTree_MouseDown(object sender,
MouseEventArgs e)
    {
        System.Windows.Forms.TreeView tv =
(System.Windows.Forms.TreeView)sender;
        System.Windows.Forms.TreeNode n = tv.GetNodeAt(e.X,
e.Y);
        System.Windows.Forms.TreeNode childNode;
        System.Data.DataTable dt;
        System.Data.DataRow dRow;
        string[] values;
        int i;

        if (n != null && n.Level == 0)
        {
           n.Nodes.Clear();

           values = n.Tag.ToString().Split('_');

           if (int.Parse(values[1]) > 0)//node has sublevels
           {
             if (!n.IsExpanded)
             {
               dt = fill in data table;

               for (i = 0; i < dt.Rows.Count; i++)
               {
                 dRow = dt.Rows[i];
```

```
            childNode = new
System.Windows.Forms.TreeNode();
            childNode.Tag = string.Format("{0}_0",
dRow["ID"]);//ID_hasChildren
            childNode.Text = dRow["Desc"].ToString();

          n.Nodes.Add(childNode);
        }
      }
      else
      {
          n.Nodes.Clear();

          childNode = new System.Windows.Forms.TreeNode();
          n.Nodes.Add(childNode);
      }
    }
  }
}
```

What am I doing wrong?

A: You described a bug and it is exactly doing what you coded it to do:

"...but it would clear the child nodes and add one blank text node..."

Code:

```
      {
          n.Nodes.Clear();

          childNode = new System.Windows.Forms.TreeNode();
          n.Nodes.Add(childNode);
      }
```

In pseudo-code, your code says when a node has 'children' and the node is not expanded, then clear all 'children' and add a blank one.

So every time you try to collapse a node that has 'sublevels', this code will be executed. You should first check whether or not the node is expanded. If it is, then collapse it. If it's not, then do other checks like whether or not 'children' must be added to it.

I'm also assuming you are doing this because perhaps you have so many nodes to fill that you do not want the performance hit when filling all of them at once.

I suggest that you fill all first 'child' nodes with the data they are supposed to get, and capture the "BeforeExpand" event to fill the rest of the data when expanded (alternatively you could use a blank first 'child' node as you are doing).

Once you have filled the data for the first time, you can leave it. There's no need to delete it, there is no performance benefit in deleting it.

This would save you all the trouble you are encountering, unless of course your reasons are far different than what I am assuming.

You can also use the "BeforeExpand" (load child nodes) and "BeforeCollapse" (unload child nodes). The "TreeViewCancelEventArgs" contains the node that triggers the event.

The following is another situation that can give you another approach to your problem:

The program that was used for this was for a 'ticket view' for something like 'support tickets' but for graphic arts. The database contained the 'ticket number table', and a table for the postings (many postings per ticket relationship).

You can fill the 'dataset' with the ticket numbers, and use one 'child' node for the subject of the ticket. These were in the same 'datarow'. You can fill the other 'child' node with information about the originating post (Name of person, phone number, etc). So after the expansion, query your database for the postings and fill the rest of the 'child' nodes with data from the first posting.

Code:

```
TICKET#1
 |-- Ticket Subject
 |-- John Smith
 |-- Phone# 555-5555
```

So it isn't difficult, it's just how your data is structured and what you use for that first node.

Question 20: NetIntruder (MIS){XE "NetIntruder (MIS)"}

I'm trying to figure out how to use an ".exe" file in my project, specifically "Robocopy.exe" from the Windows Resource kit. Now, I want this to be included in the project so that the resource kit does not have to be installed to the machine where the tool is run, but I'm having some difficulty. I've added "robocopy.exe" as an embedded resource, but I'm not sure how to actually call the executable and pass arguments to it.

How can I start this up?

A: You don't need to include the 'exe' in your project.

Take it back out and then use "System.Diagnostics.Process" to launch the app with some arguments.

```
System.Diagnostics.Process p = new Process();

p.StartInfo.FileName = "robocopy.exe";
p.StartInfo.Arguments = "yourargumentsinastring";
p.Start();
```

If you place "RoboCopy.exe" in your project directory, you can then include it within your project output by doing the following:

Go to top of project and click on the "Show All Files".

You should see the "robocopy.exe" as a white file icon in your project.

Right-click and choose "include in project".

Go to 'properties' of the file and choose 'Build Action' "None" and 'Copy' to 'Output Directory' as "Copy if Newer".

Now, you can use what was suggested except that:

Code:

```
p.StartInfo.FileName = "robocopy.exe";
```

It should really be changed to:

Code:

```
p.StartInfo.FileName =
Directory.GetCurrentDirectory()+@"\robocopy.exe";
```

What all this does is copy the "robocopy.exe" to where your project gets placed. In the case you are compiling it, it will be placed where the 'exe' for your application ends up.

If you include your project in a setup project, it will get placed in the same directory your 'exe' goes when someone uses the installer.

Your application then expects the "robocopy.exe" to be in the same directory your app is located, and calls it as a separate application.

You cannot wrap an 'exe' within an 'exe' and expect it to run. Keep in mind that with this method, you really cannot use the "robocopy.exe" with any other application or stand-alone unless the user knows it exists in your app directory.

In the case the user already has the kit installed, you are merely doubling the amount of space it is taking up. This isn't a big deal really if your app is accustomed for maybe a few people, but is considered a bad practice if it were say a much larger external application you were trying to call (mb of files) and distributing your app to many people. In those cases, you should really install the "robocopy.exe" as it was intended either from your installer or with the regular distribution only because it does not promote the idea of installing multiple copies for the sake of ease on programming.

Question 21: C# with block

What is the C# equivalent of the VB "With...End With" block?

A: There is no direct comparison. "With...End" is for short handing code{XE "short handing code"}, not for making better applications.

Try to check-out the following site:

http://www.harding.edu/USER/fmccown/WWW/vbnet_csharp _comparison.html#objects

Define a short name variable and set it like the following:

```
dataset d = xxx.xxxxx.xxx.xxxx
int32 nRows = d.Tables(0).Rows
```

If you have a long dotted string of methods/properties off a variable, you can create another variable to point to the last of them, which becomes easier to use.

Question 22: studio.net

Visual Basic 6.0 and previous had an immediate window where you could type commands while in debug mode.

Did visual 'studio.net' do away with that?

Or is it just called something different?

How would I get to it from the menus?

A: It is in there. Hit "Ctrl+Alt+I" and you will get it.

> Debug--> Windows --> Immediate

Question 23: Splitting a string into 250 characters

I have a large string, say maybe 1,000 characters long and I want to split the string into 250 characters. So, I will have:

str = 1000 chars long

Do the split:

str1 = 250 chars long
str2 = 250 chars long
str3 = 250 chars long

etc.

How can I do this?

A: You could just get the length of the string and substring it in 250 character chunks. It wouldn't be that difficult of a code piece to write for any dynamic string length. But, there is probably an easier way of doing it.

You can try the following code:

```
Code:
int i = 0;
int index = 0;
int len = srcString.Length;
if (len >= 250)
{
  while (i < len - 250)
  {
    destStrings[index] = srcString.Substring(i, 250);
    i += 250;
    index++;
  }
}
// pick up any remainder
if (len % 250 > 0)
{
  index++;
```

```
    destStrings[index] = srcString.Substring(i)
}
```

The 'Split method' wouldn't help in this case, as you don't have a 'delimiter' to split on. So, you have to do it the hard way.

Note that these are characters, not bytes.

There is a suggestion but I do not like the way it handles the "newline \n", or the "tab \t". You can use 5 just for testing.

Code:
```
using System;
using System.Text.RegularExpressions;
namespace regexsplitpattern
{
    class MainClass
    {
        public static void Main(string[] args)
        {
            string input = "12a\t3412b3412c3412d3412e341\n2";
            MatchCollection mc;
            Regex regex = new
Regex("(.{5}|.+)",RegexOptions.Singleline);
            mc = regex.Matches(input);
            for (int i = 0; i < mc.Count; i++)
            {
                Console.WriteLine("value " + mc[i].Value);
            }
        }
    }
}
results
value 12a      3
value 412b3
value 412c3
value 412d3
value 412e3
value 41
2
```

Question 24: Explanation of a code

What is the explanation of this code?

this.myTimer.Tick += new
System.EventHandler(this.myTimer_Tick);

How do I mark this thread as 'resolved'?

A: "System.Windows.Forms.Timer Control" is essentially a new thread that notifies you on regular intervals. Its notification happens through an event called "Tick".

So, when you say "mytimer.Tick += new EventHandler(this.mytimer_Tick)", you are subscribing to that event. You say, "when your time (interval) has elapsed, I want to know about it".

When the timer ticks, it calls:

```
private void mytimer_Tick(object sender, EventArgs e)
{
   //and this is where you do the work that happens every interval
(Timer Tick)
}
```

The other thing that might be causing confusion is the "+=" operator. These two lines are equivalent.

Code:
```
a = a + b;
a += b;
```

In the case of events, this operator subscribes you to the event. You can also remove yourself with the "-=" operator.

Question 25: Plug-in based development

I'm going to build an application that should be based on 'plug-in' that extends the core application with extra customer specific functions.

I like my plug-in to have a common look, feel, and behavior. I like tips on how to design my application to make it expandable. I like some tips on design patterns that could be useful.

I like to see my core-application as a framework for further development of plug-ins. I've read some articles on 'reflection' and I get the point of it, but I don't really yet have the right thinking of how to apply common design patterns.

My other question is how I can get the look and feel of my plug-in dialogs like 'Visual Studios' dock able windows?

Is there any support for that in the '.NET' framework?

A: The 2.0 Framework contains a lot of those dock able controls. You can also purchase them from other third party companies.

In terms of plug-in, you generally create a separate project that contains only interfaces or a base class type, generally 'interface' is better.

That project can be compiled as a class library (DLL), where other projects can use to create their own compatible DLL's. I tend to take each of these DLL's and put them into a specific folder. Then, get all the files from that folder and create a specific instance of each item.

For example, say I'm writing a drawing application. The application contains "tools" which are used to draw things on the screen. So, you might create an interface in your separate project called "iDrawingTool".

In another project called "RectangleTools", you would create a "Rectangle Tool class" that uses the "iDrawingTool" interface.

Compile the DLL and stick it into a "Tools" folder in your main projects 'bin' directory (or anywhere common for that matter).

When you're drawing application loads, you'll find all the tools in the 'Tools' folder and create instances of "iDrawingTool" (Activator.GetInstance(...)).

Now, your application is purely a framework and will only be functional if there are tools available in that folder. You can then distribute other tools very easily over time. Just create a new project and develop the new tool. When it's done, drop it in the 'tools' directory and you're done.

In terms of design patterns, ensure that you are using 'Model View' controller wherever possible. This allows your code to be manageable and scalable.

I hope that gets you started. If you're notifying all plug-ins of a tool change, then you could use MVC or some other type of "Subscriber" pattern. But, I personally prefer to keep reference to all plug-ins accessible in my controller.

Question 26: C# file list box

I am using a 'filelistbox' in a c# program ("openfiledialog" doesn't work for me) and I need to have the ability to count how many items are contained in the listbox.

I have:

```
string[] flbItems =
Directory.GetFiles(this.strSourcePath);
```

which should give me an array that contains every file.

Then, I have:

```
for (int x = 0; x < flbItems.GetLength(1); x++)
```

which should loop as many times as there are files. These two things do not seem to work though, the program just crashes with no error message.

What I am trying to do (say, I have these files):

```
45445423.tif
42323455.jpg
43214141.png
44232442h.gif
adddddcq.pdf
```

I need to be able to remove all files that contain a non-numeric character. So, the "44232442h.gif" and "adddddcq.pdf" should stay, but I want to remove the rest.

How can I loop through the items in the 'filelistbox' to check them, and remove files that shouldn't be shown?

A: You can try the following:

```
string[] flbItems = Directory.GetFiles(this.strSourcePath);

for (int i = 0; i < flbItems.Length, i++)
{
```

```
  string item =
System.IO.Path.GetFileNameWithoutExtension(flbItems[i]);

  if (String.IsNumeric(item))
  {
    listbox1.Items .Add(item);
  }
}
```

int totalfiles = listbox1.Items.Count;

It may be part of 2.0 Framework.

In 1.1 I believe you can make a reference to the VB6 dll, or you can write your own method where you check each individual character to see if it is numeric or not.

Question 27: Losing 3KB when Writing

I am reading then writing to a file. I have a 4GB file that I am processing. The resulting file is missing 3KB. I am having a problem comparing the files because it is so big.

Here is my code:

```
StreamReader reader = new StreamReader(file_name,
Encoding.UTF8, false, 100000);
    StreamWriter converted_file = new
StreamWriter(file_name_out, false, Encoding.UTF8, 100000);
    converted_file.AutoFlush = true;
    while (!reader.EndOfStream)
    {
       converted_file.Write(reader.ReadLine());
    }

    reader.Close();
    reader.Dispose();
    converted_file.Flush();
    converted_file.Close();
    converted_file.Dispose();
```

I have used this on a 400MB file and there was no loss of data.

Is there a solution for this?

A: You might also want to look at possible differences in how 'line-separators' are being handled. You can read in by 'carriage returns' and writing out with none. Now, the file sizes are the same.

Check if the size you are looking at is the actual size of the files, not "size on disk" which is sometimes shown. Since files are usually stored in blocks of 4k, a variance of less than 4k can be expected with regards to size on disk.

Also, just to be on the safe side, move the "reader.close" and "reader.dispose" to after the "Flush()".

Question 28: Create updates

I made a 'Setup Project' in Visual Studio 2005 for my application. All works well, but when I'm going to distribute an update in a new build version of my application, my clients have to first uninstall my application and then reinstall the new one.

I get the following error when I try to install my app again:

"Another version of this product is already installed. Installation of this version cannot continue. To configure or remove the existing version of this product, use Add/Remove Programs on the Control Panel."

What should I do to make the new release be installed over the old one?

A: You need to increment the version number of your application. Then, it will install as you want it to.

Visual Studio has stopped auto-incrementing after version 6, though there is a code on the web for restoring that functionality.

The procedure might be similar to Visual Studio 2005.

Select your 'Setup Project', and then look at the 'properties' window. There should be a property called "Version". Increment it in the fashion that makes sense for the changes you've made.

Do your 'build' and 'deploy' stuff, and then you should be all set.

Question 29: Icon shows as an icon with no picture

I have been working on an application for some time, but now I am testing deployment. I find that the icon shows ok as a shortcut on the desktop but not in the 'start' menu where it looks like a VS icon with no color. I have also noticed that if I use a small icon (16x16), the program has a good icon (correct picture) if viewed in a folder on detail view. But if I switch to 'tiles view', then the icon looks bad (like there has been no picture drawn on it) and vice versa if I use 32x32. I want my program to show the correct icon no matter how it is viewed.

How can I do that?

A: You need to create an icon file that contains multiple icon formats. Take a look at "Axialis Icon studio". An icon file can contain more than 1 icon.

Typically an icon file will contain the following:

Full Color Alpha Blended Windows XP Icons
Full Color (Not alpha blended)
256 Colors
8 Colors
and Monochrome icons at the following sizes:

16x16
22x22
32x32
48x48
72x72

This allows the 'OS' or software to choose the most applicable icon for its display needs.

The file extension of this file is ".ico".

Question 30: Binding data textbox format

I'm binding a text box to a 'Currency data type'{XE "'Currency data type'"} in a Microsoft Access database. Everything works as expected except for the format of the 'currency field' in the text box. I want to display 2 decimal places like "#.##".

No matter what I enter or routines I add, it will work to append ".oo" to the text box string even when the value is dollars. The binding seems to strip away any zeros.

10.10 became 10.1, 20.00 became 20.

Any ideas how I can solve this?

A: Try using "0.00" instead of "#.##". I believe "#" is reserved for placeholders that are OPTIONAL, whereas "0" is used for placeholders that are REQUIRED.

When binding to the access database you must create "ConvertEventHandlers" to intercept the 'Format' and 'Parse' that occurs automatically during the binding process.

First, create a separate binding:

Binding b = new Binding("Text",dataview,"AccessDatabaseColumnName");

Then, create new "ConvertEventHandlers" for the 'Format' and 'Parse' events that occur during binding:

b.Format += new ConvertEventHandler(DecimalToCurrencyString);
b.Parse += new ConvertEventHandler(CurrencyStringToDecimal);

Then, bind the 'datacolumn' to the textbox:

TextBox1.DataBindings.Add(b);

Here are the conversion functions:

private void DecimalToCurrencyString(object sender,

```
ConvertEventArgs cevent)
{
    if(cevent.DesiredType != typeof(string)) return;
    cevent.Value = ((decimal) cevent.Value).ToString("c");
}

private void CurrencyStringToDecimal(object sender,
ConvertEventArgs cevent)
{
    if(cevent.DesiredType != typeof(decimal)) return;
    cevent.Value =
Decimal.Parse(cevent.Value.ToString(),NumberStyles.Currency, null);
}
```

Make sure to reference "System.Globalization" to cover "NumberStyles.Currency." using "System.Globalization;".

Now, a decimal field stored in an 'Access database' will convert to a 'Currency' format in a textbox.

Question 31: Selecting from list box with right mouse button

If I left click on a line item in a listbox, it selects the item. Clicking the right mouse button is detectable in the listbox but it does not select the item.

Is there a way to override this listbox behavior, and select an item with the right mouse button?

A: In your right-button event handler, set the "SelectedIndex" property for the control.

If you are having a problem determining which item was being selected when the right mouse button was clicked in the listbox control, you can solve that by adding the "listbox.TopIndex" with the 'Y' mouse position divided by the selected item's height. This will give you the item that was clicked by the right mouse button so you could assign the "SelectedIndex".

Question 32: Compiling C# project on the DOS prompt

How can I compile and execute an MDI project on the DOS prompt?

A: You can use the following:

csc /out:TargetFile.exe SourceFile.cs

csc.exe - c# compiler{XE "c# compiler"}

Question 33: Add a horizontal break line between Menu Items

I am adding the "menuitems" to the "contextMenu" of a little system tray application. I would like to add a separator between two "MenuItems".

Here is the code:

```
this.contextMenu1.MenuItems.AddRange(new
System.Windows.Forms.MenuItem[] {
this.menuItem1,          this.menuItem2,          this.menuIte
m5,          this.menuItem3,          this.menuItem4});
```

 I have tried:

```
menuItem.BreakLine = true;
```

but that adds a vertical break and creates 2 columns of my 'popupmenu'.

How can I tell it to put a horizontal separator between 2 "MenuItems"?

A: Try something like adding a "-" to the value of a menu item, just like adding "Open" or "Exit" under the "File" menu;
.menuItem("-");

Question 34: Reading XML file and exporting onto an Access db

I'm trying to build an application which basically needs to read in an XML document, extract the necessary data, export it an Access database, and ultimate product of 'Crystal Report' from the information on the database.

The XML document is very large, and the "wanted" data are spread out across the nested XML tags.

How do I go about grabbing only the data that I want, and then exporting those data on appropriate fields on an Access table?

I'm using C# for this. I'm looking at ".Net libraries" called: 'XPath', 'XmlNodeReader', and 'XmlDataDocument'. In conjunction, these seems to do what I want, but how would I go about grabbing the elements that I want and insert them onto the appropriate fields inside the Access table?

Do I actually need an Access database to produce the Crystal Report in the first place?

A: The general idea is to use "XmlValidatingReader" object along with "XmlTextReader" object to read your file a little bit at a time. For each node that gets read (and the node could one be of several different types - elements, attributes, comments, etc) you would append it to a 'StringBuffer' (see the example for "XmlValidatingReader.Read" method in the ".NET" help).

When you see that you get the end element node for your XML record (like </Customer>), you would then load it into a "XmlDocument" object via the 'Load method' (one of its overloads takes a String), and then use 'XPath' queries against your document to extract the elements you're interested in, and write them to your Access database.

Question 35: Defining collections

I can't understand some things about defining collections.

Here is an example:

```
public class Animals:CollectionBase
{
  public void Add(Animal NewAnimal);
  {
    List.Add(newAnimal);
  }

}
```

How can "CollectionBase" class implement "IList" interface if it doesn't implement all of "IList's" methods? How is that possible?

'List property' returns a variable of type "IList", which points to an object from which this 'List property' was called from? Am I right?

How can I use "List.Add()" method if I haven't defined it yet? Where is this method defined?

A: If you derive a class from some base, the methods provided by the base are automatically derived as well unless you override them. Then, your methods take precedence. C#'s inheritance model is similar to C++'s.

You can see a list of all of the base members (if you're using 'vs.net') by typing this. Inside of a function and all of the members of the class will appear in a drop down box.

You can also try the follo wing:

```
public class animallist : CollectionBase
{
  //setup the class by calling base constructor and setting inner list
(derived from collection base) to a new array list
  public animallist() : base()
  {
```

```
    this.InnerLIst = new ArrayList();
  }
  //overloaded constructor is not necessary
  public animallist(ArrayList l) : base()
  {
    this.InnerList = l;
  }
```

//don't let user see Ilist implementation...force them to use array list provided by CollectionBase derived class (this is actually a 3rd level class)

```
  protected override IList List;

  public void Add(animal a) //define this yourself
  {
    this.InnerList.Add(a);  //InnerList is derived property
  }

  public animal Get(int i)
  {
    return (animal)this.InnerList; //make the class useful by being able to
```
extract an animal at a certain location in the array
```
  }
```

//expose the array if you want to be able to do other stuff like searching
```
  public ArrayList animal array
  {
    get {
      return InnerList;
    }
  }
}
```

Question 36: Code for testing if an "OleDbConnection" is open or close

I tried the following:

```
if(con1.State == Closed)
{
con1.Open();
}
```

That didn't worked at all.

How can I correct the syntax?

A: It should be:

```
if (con1.State == ConnectionState.Closed)
{
  con1.Open();
}
```

Personally, I think better design is called for here. You should know at any point in your code whether a connection is open. The problem is that you are probably passing around the same connection to various methods, and at some point you can't be sure what state it is in. Streamline your code so that the state is obvious, this will help with maintainability and flexibility down the road.

Question 37: Simple basic form

I have a "mainmenu(mnMain)" with a menu option "Search(mnMainSearch)" on the "main form(frmMain)". I need to know how to have an 'on click' function of the menu option of "mnMainSearch" to have the "Search form(frmSearch)" be loaded with focus. "frmMain" is still in the background with out focus.

How can I execute that?

A: You still can double click on the menu item to open the 'code' window. Then, you need to make an instance of your search form like the following:

```
frmSearch fs = new frmSearch();
fs.Show();
```

Question 38: Casting & WMI Problem

I keep getting a casting exception in the following section of the code. I can't seem to convert from the 'object' to 'int'.

Is there any way of getting the first element from "queryCollection" other than having to enumerate through it?

```
ManagementObjectCollection queryCollection = query.Get();
    int tempint;
    Object obj;
foreach(ManagementObject mo in queryCollection)
    {

        obj = mo.InvokeMethod("Terminate", null);
here---------->tempint = (int) obj;
          return tempint;
        }
```

A: The best way to do conversions is to utilize the 'Convert' class. In your case, you can do something like this:

```
        tempint = Convert.ToInt32(obj);
```

For more information, check 'help' for the 'Convert' class.

Question 39: ADO

Is it possible to create an Access DB "on the fly"using ADO?

If not, is there any other method?

A: You can use ADOX (COM) objects to do it. See ADOX API Reference in MSDN library for more details.

Question 40: Show result to a label

I come from a C++ builder environment and I was convinced to try C#. So I tried to rewrite a simple old program from c++ to c#. That's what I've done so far. It compiles perfectly but does not work at all.

```
private void button1_Click(object sender, System.EventArgs e)
    {
        double xz = Convert.ToDouble(textBox1.Text);
        double yz = Convert.ToDouble(textBox2.Text);
        double yx = Convert.ToDouble(textBox3.Text);
        double xx = Convert.ToDouble(textBox4.Text);
        double yy = Convert.ToDouble(textBox5.Text);
        double xy = Convert.ToDouble(textBox6.Text);
        double dxxz,dxyz,dyxz,dyyz, b1, b2,x0, y0, c, lx,ly, lz;
        dxxz = xx - xz;
        dxyz = xy - xz;
        dyxz = yx - yz;
        dyyz = yy - yz;
        b1 = yx * dyyz + xx * dxyz;
        b2 = yy * dyxz + xy * dxxz;
        x0 = (b1 * dyxz - b2 * dyyz)/(dyxz * dxyz + dyyz * dxxz);
        y0 = (b1 * dxxz - b2 * dxyz)/(dyxz * dxyz + dyyz * dxxz);
        c = Math.Sqrt(-(xx -x0) * (xy -x0) - (yx -y0) * (yy - y0));
        lx = Math.Sqrt(Math.Pow(xx-x0,2)+ (yx - y0) +
Math.Pow(c,2));
        ly = Math.Sqrt(Math.Pow(xy-x0,2)+ (yy - y0) +
Math.Pow(c,2));
        lz = Math.Sqrt(Math.Pow(xz-x0,2)+ (yz - y0) +
Math.Pow(c,2));
        x0= Convert.ToDouble(label27.Text);
        y0= Convert.ToDouble(label28.Text);
```

Is there a solution for this?

A: Try reversing the assignment at the end. Instead of:

```
x0= Convert.ToDouble(label27.Text);
y0= Convert.ToDouble(label28.Text);
```

Try:
```
label27.Text = x0.ToString();
label28.Text = y0.ToString();
```

Question 41: Saving the properties of a class

I made a new class with a lot of data. Now, I want to save this class data to a file. How should I "attack" this problem?

Do I have to write each and every property data of the class to a file, or can I save the whole class in go?

What is the best way to save a file for security reasons? I don't want a text file.

A: What you are trying to do is called "serialization", and you can find it very easily in MSDN online.

Basically, you mark your class with the "Serialized" attribute, and then use something like this:

```
MyObject obj = new MyObject();
IFormatter formatter = new BinaryFormatter();
Stream stream = new FileStream("MyFile.bin", FileMode.Create,
FileAccess.Write, FileShare.None);
formatter.Serialize(stream, obj);
stream.Close();
```

There are some other formatters available, including an XML.

If you want a safer way, you can use crypt streams to write data. ".NET" framework supports different encrypting methods, both symmetric and asymmetric, like RSA for example.

Question 42: Using a class in a code

I am developing a web application using VS.Net and C#. I understand how to use other system objects such as database communication.

Now, I have written my own class, and "VS.Net" created the namespace "GabeC". My class is called "ComFuncs". I have a "ComFuncs" constructor, and a public string is "Open(int myVariable)" function.

I am having trouble on understanding how I can use this class and function from my "default.aspx.cs" page.

I don't understand how VS.Net and C# know where to find "ComFunc". For example, I use VB 6.0 quite a bit and if I write a dll called "ComFuncs", and before I can use it (early bind it any way) I need to add it as a reference to the project. In C#, before I can use ADO, I need to add something like using "System.Data.SqlClient;" at the top of the class. I guess I assume that since "System.Data.SqlClient;" is a system object VS.Net knows where to find it.

I want to create an object that handles all my database work for me so I can use it in multiple applications. If I create a DLL or class (which should I be doing?) in a project of its own, how do I use it in my other projects?

A: You need to instantiate a copy of your class:

    ComFuncs MyComFuncs = new ComFuncs();

And then, to call your method:

    String Result = MyComFuncs.isOpen(42)

A way to remember things like this is to think of the class as a cookie cutter that stamps out (instantiates) objects that you can use.

In your visual studio project window, expand the "References" section. Right click, and select "Add | Reference". Once you've done that, you can insert the "Using blah.blah" statement at the top of your code.

Question 43: Screen size

I simply need to get the screen size.

I remember in VB, it goes like "screen.width & screen.height..".

How can I do that?

A: You can use "Screen.Bounds.Width" and "Screen.Bounds.Height".

Question 44: Adding a new "XmlNode" to a file

How can I add a new node to an existing xml -file?

XmlNode -class has a method "AppendChild(XmlNode node)", but I can't create a new node (XmlNode newNode = new XmlNode()) because "XmlNode" is an abstract class.

Is there some way to create a new node?

A: Try this:

XmlNode newElem = doc.CreateNode(XmlNodeType.Element, "NodeName", "");

You can also create an element like this:

XmlElement newElem = doc.CreateElement("NodeName");

You can also take a look at MS help for more information:

//MS.VSCC/MS.MSDNVS/cpref/html/frlrfSystemXmlXmlDocu mentClassCreateElementTopic.htm

Question 45: Accessing labels on form

I have a windows form called "Main"with a label call "lProgress". I also have a Component called "Export".

Inside "Export" I have a function "PopulateData".

On button click in main, I call the "PopulateData" function.

```
public void PopulateData()
{
   int uBound = Sectors.GetUpperBound(0);
   int j = 0;
   while( j <= uBound )
      {
        //Somehow Main.lProgress.Text = j;
      }
}
```

How can I access this label in these circumstances?

A: You can pass the label as a parameter to "PopulateData()".

Question 46: Type or name space error message

I am creating my first Project in C#. My objective is to create a GUI that will interact with the SQL server db. I have created 'Client' project, so far so good.
I added a project 'DataAccess' that includes all classes that do the connection to the db.

Now, my problem is to connect between the 'client' and the 'DataAccess' projects. In the Client side I added: Using DataAccess.Connection.

Building the solution raised an error:

"The type or namespace name 'DataAccess' could not be found (are you missing a using directive or an assembly reference?)".

How can I connect with 'DataAccess' project?

A: You need to add a reference to the 'DataAccess' project, there are two ways to do this.

This presumes you have built the 'DataAccess' project which should be a "Class Library" project. When you build a class library, it creates a DLL in the Debug or Release directory.

If you don't expect to make changes to 'DataAccess', you can add a reference to your solution by right clicking on 'References' in the 'Solution View' and choose 'Add Reference' from the menu.

This brings up the "Add Reference" form. Click the "Browse" button on the right and navigate to the 'DataAccess' project directory and find the "DataAccess.dll" in the Debug or Release directory. You still have to put the "using DataAccess" in your code.

The second way to do this is to add the 'DataAccess' project to your 'Client' project

In the Solution Explorer view, right click the "Client Solution" at the top of the tree. A menu should appear. Select "Add... > Existing Project".

Navigate to the "DataAccess" project and add it to your Client solution.

On the main menu, Project > Add Reference, brings up the same 'Add Reference' form in the prior e-mail.
Now, choose the "Projects" tab at the top. Your newly added project should appear. Select it, click select on the right, and then 'OK' at the bottom. You are set to roll.

You still need to add "using DataAccess" if you don't want to explicitly refer to the namespace.

Question 47: C# exception

I heard that using exceptions in C++ sometimes causes unpredictable results, even suspending the system. Rarely of course, but it can be destructing in cases of business project.

The alternative is writing a module for error handling not using exceptions at all, this is a more difficult way.

Were there any tweaks done in '.NET' (C#) with exceptions, perhaps making them less dangerous to use and more reliable?

Is there a short overview of exception difficulties in use and possible errors concerning them?

A: Exceptions are much better integrated into the .NET environment. No more having to choose between Win32 exceptions and C++ exceptions (neither of which were that fun to work with).

I've pretty much decided that exceptions are there to catch programmer errors, not user errors. If a user supplies bad input, then my code should have caught it. If a network resource is unavailable, or if the database connect string is wrong, then an exception should catch it.

One thing that is a little unusual in .NET exceptions is that the variable scope spans the try, catch, and finally blocks. So you can't do something like this:

```
try {
   SqlConnection MyConnect = new SqlConnection(connectString);
} catch (Exception e) {
   MessageBox.Show(e.Message);
}
MyConnect.Close();
```

because the compiler will complain about no instance of MyConnect being found for the Close method. Do something like this:

```
SqlConnection MyConnect = null;
try {
```

```
  MyConnect = new SqlConnection(connectString);
} catch (Exception e) {
  MessageBox.Show(e.Message);
}
MyConnect.Close();
```

Or even better, move the 'Close' call into a 'Finally' section. There will be a n instance.

The exception handling in ".NET" is very reliable, as it's used by the framework itself. So any "problems" would have appeared very quickly during its development.

Using 'try..catch..finally' blocks have very little performance impact, but throwing an exception (whether by you using the throw function, or a system-generated exception) is expensive. So handle exceptions as soon as you can.

Question 48: Version info

Is it possible to have the version info of an application which is found in "AssemblyInfo.cs" printed on the screen?

Is it possible to retrieve Version info from "AssemblyInfo.cs" at runtime?

A: Yes, you use the "LoadFrom" method of the Assembly object:

ms-help://MS.VSCC/MS.MSDNVS/cpref/html/frlrfSystemReflectionAssemblyClassLoadFromTopic.htm

Once you have an Assembly object, call the "GetName" method, which returns an "AssemblyName" object. This object has a Version property which returns a Version object. The Version object has major and minor properties.

Question 49: Succinct way to write multiple case values

Is there a more succinct way of writing the following?

```
select (myInt)
{
case 1:
case 2:
case 3:
...
```

Perhaps as:

```
select(myInt)
{
case 1, 2, 3:
...
```

A: The C# language defines it like this:

```
switch (expression)
{
  case constant-expression: :
    statement
    jump-statement
  [default:
    statement
    jump-statement]
}
```

For "constant-expression:" (note the colon!), it says "Control is transferred to a specific case according to the value of this expression." There's no mention of a range of values or a list of expressions.

Question 50: Make a button the "default" on a form

When I add buttons to a dialog in VC++, I can designate one as the default which will receive a click message when 'Return' is pressed on any control.

Where's its counterpart in C# forms?

A: There's a property on the form called "AcceptButton". Set it to the button you want to be the default.

You can also assign a button to the "CancelButton" property, which does what you expect.

Question 51: System.Math

How can I use 'Trig Functions' in C#?

The only thing I can find is using " System.Math", but I can't figure out where to put it or how to use it. In "framework.net" docs, it says to put "Imports System.Math" at the beginning of the program. But I must be doing something wrong because I cannot get it to work.

How can I make it work?

A: Math is a class, not a namespace. It's actually part of the System namespace, so more than likely you don't have to reference/use any additional namespaces.

If you look at the member info for the Math class (ms-help://MS.VSCC/MS.MSDNVS/cpref/html/frlrfsystemmathmemberstopic.htm), you'll see a yellow "S" beside all the public methods. That means that you don't have instantiate (create an instance of) class Math in order to use them. They're "Static".

So the Pythagorean theorem would be:

```
double SideALength, SideBLength;
double HypotenuseLength;
SideALength = 3.0;
SideBLength = 4.0;
HypotenuseLength = Math.Sqrt((SideALength * SideALength) +
(SideBLength * SideBLength));
If (double.IsNaN(HypotenuseLength) {
  // Something bad happened
}
```

Note that I'm using the static method "IsNaN" off the double class to determine if something went wrong in the square root method (you should always check return values).

Question 52: Passing info between forms

When a user selects something on a form, I want to pop up a window with four text boxes that they can enter information into, and click a button that sends the information back to the original form.

What is the best approach to take?

A: Create the pop up form with the four fields on it, and an 'OK' and 'Cancel' button. Add four properties to the form to expose the values of the four text boxes.

Then, in the main form you will create an instance of the pop up, display it and then retrieve data from it when it is closed. It will look something like this in the main form:

```
MyPopupForm popup = new MyPopupForm();
popup.ShowDialog();

if (popup.DialogResult == DialogResult.OK)
{
    // Get data from the popup form
    this.txtOne = popup.FieldOne;
    this.txtTwo = popup.FieldTwo;
    // etc
}
```

Question 53: Screen Updating

I recall from VB/VBA that when working with forms, you could switch the screen updating 'off' when performing some long process, and then switch it back 'on' again.

The point being that the code would run faster as it didn't have to keep re-drawing the form. Also, the app's appearance would be better as you wouldn't be left with a 'half-drawn' form image as the processing was being carried out.

Is there something similar in C#?

A: I don't see anything in the 'Forms' class about this. You could probably do something like disable the form (using .Enable = false), update its contents, and re-enable it. Or you could probably use the traditional WinAPI method.

Another suggestion is to do the following:

"System.Windows.Forms" has two methods that can be used in tandem: "SuspendLayout()" and "ResumeLayout()".

"SuspendLayout" suppress multiple 'Layout' events while you adjust multiple attributes of the control. For example, you could call the "SuspendLayout" method, then set the Size, Location, Anchor, or Dock properties of the control. Then, call the "ResumeLayout" method to allow the changes to take effect.

Question 54: Interfaces

Can I expose properties through an interface?

For example, I created an employee class that contains 'firstName' and 'lastName' properties. Then, I created an 'IEmployee' interface that I want to expose these properties.

Is this possible or am I trying to do something that is not meant for interfaces?

A: An Interface does not expose anything. An interface is defined as a contract for a class that implements the interface. The contract states that any class that implements the interface will implement all the methods and properties defined in the interface.

Typically, an interface is used to define methods that will be used across classes, something more generic than an employee class.

This is a good website tutorial on interfaces:

http://www.devarticles.com/art/1/131/

Question 55: SQL string

I have an ASP.NET web application written in C#. When a user enters an apostrophe ('), it has a problem writing to the db because SQL uses ' in its statements. How do I get around this problem?

Is there a way to search a string and replace the ' with the ASCII code (character 39)?

A: There are a few options. One is to use stored procedures, and pass the string as a parameter. This makes the code cleaner and more secure too.

Second, is if you want to replace the character, you can use double-single quotes. For example:

```
string s;
s = "Hello World, this is a single quote '";
s = s.Replace("'", "''");
MessageBox.Show(s);
```

You can use a Unicode character which would be '\u0027'.

But I think the database will still have trouble if you do a: s = s.Replace("'", '\u0027');

For more information, in the help section of your VS.Net IDE, look up the article title "Putting Quotation Marks in a String Programmatically (Windows Forms)".

Using string replacement on these characters will work, but you'll actually see performance improvements by using ADO.NET Parameter objects. When you use them, not only do they take care of those annoying single-quotes and double-quote characters, it allows the database to store your query in its procedure cache. So the next time you run it, it doesn't have to parse it first (which can be very expensive in terms of CPU time).

To use them, do something like this:

```
public CUser GetAUser(string ConnectStringHere, int
UserIDToGetHere)
```

```
{
SqlConnection sqlConn = null;
SqlCommand sqlComm = null;
SqlDataReader sqlDR = null;
CUser MyUser = null;
StringBuilder MySQL = new StringBuilder();
try
{
  sqlConn = new SqlConnection(ConnectStringHere);

  MySQL.Append(" SELECT FirstName, LastName,");
  MySQL.Append("  UserName, Role,");
  MySQL.Append("  PhoneNumber, LastLoginDate,");
  MySQL.Append("  BadLoginCount");
  MySQL.Append(" FROM dbo.tbl_User");
  MySQL.Append(" WHERE IsActive = @ActiveFlag");
  MySQL.Append("  AND UserID = @UserID");

  sqlComm = new SqlCommand();
  sqlComm.CommandType = CommandType.Text;
  sqlComm.CommandText = MySQL.ToString();
  sqlComm.Parameters.Add("@ActiveFlag", SqlDbType.Bit).Value =
true;
  sqlComm.Parameters.Add("@UserID", SqlDbType.Int).Value =
UserIDToGetHere;
  sqlComm.Connection = sqlConn;

  sqlConn.Open();
  sqlDR = sqlComm.ExecuteReader();

  if (sqlDR.Read())
  {
    MyUser = new CUser();

    MyUser.UserId = UserIDToGetHere;
    MyUser.FirstName = sqlDR.GetString(0).Trim();
    MyUser.LastName = sqlDR.GetString(1).Trim();
    MyUser.UserName = sqlDR.GetString(2).Trim();
    MyUser.Role = sqlDR.GetString(3).Trim();
    MyUser.PhoneNumber = sqlDR.GetString(4).Trim();
    MyUser.LastLoginDate = sqlDR.GetDateTime(5);
    MyUser.BadLoginCount = sqlDR.GetInt(6);
  }
}
```

```
catch (Exception ex)
{
    Console.WriteLine(ex.Message + Environment.NewLine +
ex.StackTrace);
}
finally
{
    if (sqlDR != null)
    {
        if (!sqlDR.IsClosed)
        {
            sqlDR.Close();
        }
    }
    if (sqlConn != null)
    {
        if (sqlConn.State == ConnectionState.Open)
        {
            sqlConn.Close();
        }
        sqlConn.Dispose();
    }
    return MyUser;
}
}
```

Note that using the "dbo." prefix results in faster access as the database (I'm assuming SQL Server or MSDE) doesn't have to verify the owner of the table.

Question 56: Filtering a "DataSet" or a "DataTable"

In a method of a web application, I created a "SQLDataAdapter" and executed a stored procedure on the SQL Server from within the C# method. The corresponding query result is filled into a 'DataSet'. Now, I want to filter the result set in the same method according to some criteria like:

```
FilteredResult =
    filter (FilledDataSet or DataTable, criteria)
```

where criteria are something like:

```
select ....
from ...
where ....
.
.
.
```

Could you give me a simple example?

A: See below for two methods of filtering a 'datatable'.

```
class Test
{
    /// <summary>
    /// The main entry point for the application.
    /// </summary>
    [STAThread]
    static void Main(string[] args)
    {
        DataTable dt;
        DataRow[] drs;
        DataRow dr;

        //Create a datatable
        dt = new DataTable();
        dt.Columns.Add("Id",Type.GetType("System.Int16"));
        dt.Columns.Add("Name",System.Type.GetType("System.String"));
```

```
//Add two rows to the data table
dr = dt.NewRow();
dr["ID"]=10;
dr["Name"]="John";
dt.Rows.Add(dr);

dr = dt.NewRow();
dr["ID"]=11;
dr["Name"]="Bobski";
dt.Rows.Add(dr);

//Filter using the datatable select which returns an array of
datarows
//load the array of data roes with all rows with an ID = 10
drs = dt.Select("id = 11");

Console.WriteLine("Using datatable select");
Console.WriteLine("ID={0} and
Name={1}",drs[0]["ID"].ToString(),drs[0]["Name"] );
//Line below causes error because select only returns one
row
//Console.WriteLine("ID={0} and
Name={1}",drs[1]["ID"].ToString(),drs[1]["Name"] );

//Filter Using the
dt.DefaultView.RowFilter = "id=11";
Console.WriteLine("Using a view on the datatable");
Console.WriteLine("ID={0} and
Name={1}",dt.DefaultView[0]["ID"].ToString(),dt.DefaultView[0]["N
ame"] );
//Line Below causes error as the dataview only contains one
row
//Console.WriteLine("ID={0} and
Name={1}",dt.DefaultView[1]["ID"].ToString(),dt.DefaultView[1]["N
ame"] );

String Ret;
Ret=Console.ReadLine();

    }
}
```

A data set holds a collection of 'datatables', you do not need to use a 'dataset' unless you intend to create in memory relationships between 'datatables'.

Question 57: "FileInfo.Name()"

C# names a method as "FileInfo.Name{get}", what's the 'get' about? If I call "FileInfo.Name()", it throws a compiler error.

I try:

```
<code>
   FileInfo fi = new FileInfo("C:\readme.txt");
   Console.Write(fi.Name());
</code>
```

and get:

```
<code>
Hello.cs(13,19): error CS0118: 'System.IO.FileSys
     'property' where a 'method' was expected</code>
```

Is there any way to correct this?

A: By appending () to the end of 'Name', you are invoking a method rather than trying to get a property.

Try this:

```
<code>
   FileInfo fi = new FileInfo("C:\readme.txt");
   Console.Write(fi.Name);
</code>
```

Question 58: Combo box

I have bound my combo box to 'database' using "Dataset" as:

```
DataSet ds=new DataSet();
ds=data.ReturnAll(sqlstr);
cboCategory.DataSource=ds.Tables[0];
cboCategory.ValueMember="CategoryID";
cboCategory.DisplayMember="Category";
```

It is filling the 'combox' satisfactorily.

When I am trying to get an item, I do as follow:

```
Object selectedItem = cboCategory.SelectedItem;
MessageBox.Show(selectedItem.ToString());
```

It returns "System.Data.RowView" and I don't know why.

How can I get the text of the combox?
How can I get the index of the item bound in the combox?

The combox shows a list of 'strings' and I select one. Why it should be different in VB.net, ASP.net, and C#.net?

A: The selected item is an object, not the string displayed. The ".ToString" is returning correctly as it doesn't know what particular item to return, and thus is returning the type. Try casting a text box to an object and see what that returns in the "ToString" method.

You are after the string contained within the bound column within that object. What you need to do is extract it. As you are using a bound datatable, you can use something along the lines of the following:

System.Data.Datarow selectedItem = (System.Data.Datarow)
cboCategory.SelectedItem;

Question 59: "System.NullReferenceException"

I am trying to develop a component for database access. I am writing a class object where I create a new connection and command objects in the constructor, and try to use those declared objects in different methods in the class. It goes something like this:

```
namespace <namespace>
{
  public class DataObj
  {
    private SqlConnection oConn;
    private SqlCommand oCmd;

    public DataObj
    {
      SqlConnection oConn = new SqlConnection();
    SqlCommand oCmd = new SqlCommand();
    }

    public void OpenConnection()
    {
    oConn.ConnectionString = <Connection str>;
      oConn.Open();
    oCmd.Connection = oConn;
    }

  }
}
```

I get an error in the "OpenConnection" method when trying to use "oConn.Open". The error states that the object has not been instantiated.

How can I correct that?

A: The problem is with your constructor. First, your have missed the brackets of the constructor name. Second, and more importantly (as it is not pointed out be the syntax checker) by placing the type names in front of the variable names in the constructor, you are declaring them as local variables so the members are not being set.

Try the following:

```
public DataObj
    {
        //The extra type declarations mean that local variables were being
declared
        //SqlConnection oConn = new SqlConnection();
        oConn = new SqlConnection();

        //SqlCommand oCmd = new SqlCommand();
        oCmd = new SqlCommand();
    }
```

Question 60: TreeView - visible selected

When I click on a tree node, it becomes selected and goes blue (blue for most people). I can select a node with a code with something like "treeView.selectedNode = fantasticNode", which would leave "fantasticNode" highlighted.

However, when I select a node using a code before a user has clicked on the "treeView", I find that (although the node is selected) it isn't highlighted.

How can I force my "TreeView" to highlight the selected node?

A: There are two possible ways:

1. Type "treeView1.Focus();" before you select the node.
2. Type "treeView1.Select();" before you select the node.

I don't know the difference between them. It seems they do the same.

Question 61: Arraylist containing nodes

I have an array list containing a number of 'NodeInfo' objects. Node information is made up of some 'primitives', and a windows component I designed called 'PreviewBox'.

'Preview box' extends 'PictureBox'. It is a drag able and resizable item that displays certain information relative to my project.

> main form > array list of node info > preview box

I want to put a method in the code for my main form, the class that my array list is found within. That is triggered by an event such as my preview box being clicked.

I already have a method within preview box, but I don't know how to extend it in a main form for every object in an unknown amount of objects.

How would I go about this?

A: Very simple. If you choose to write a code for an event raising, you usually double click on the event at the 'events list', and then the editor adds an empty method like:

```
private void button1_Click(object sender, System.EventArgs e)
{
// here you write the action
}
```

If you look at the hidden code with its headline:

> Windows Form Designer generated code

You will see the function:

> private void InitializeComponent()

In this function you will see a row like this:

> this.button1.Click += new

System.EventHandler(this.button1_Click);

The only thing you need is to do it yourself.

You can do this function:

```
private PictureBox InitPicture(PictureBox pic)
{
    pic = new PictureBox();
    pic.Click += new System.EventHandler(ClickPic);
    pic.MouseHover += new EventHandler(pic_MouseHover);
    return pic;
}
```

In the main code, have a 'PictureBox' array. Allocate a new size to the array, and in for a loop, write:

```
pictures[i] = InitPicture(pictures[i]);
```

Now, every 'PictureBox' created will have the behavior as written for the events 'Click' and 'MouseHover'.

Question 62: Executing other programs from C#/.NET

I am writing a program in C# using Visual Studio .NET. I want my program to start other existing programs. The other programs are either MS-DOS batch files or normal (non-managed) EXE files. I am running all this under Windows XP.

Can you tell me how to start/spawn (a) another managed (.NET) program and (b) other non-managed EXE or '.bat' files from a program running inside the '.NET' framework?

A: You can start another program (managed and unmanaged) via the "Process.Start()" method in the "System.Diagnostics" namespace. You have to fill out a "ProcessStartInfo" class, where you specify the path to the executable to run, arguments to be passed on the command-line to the other program, whether to redirect the studio file handles (StandardInput, StandardOutput, and StandardError), and you can set the working directory for the new process.

Once the new process is started (the call to 'Start' returns another instance of the Process class), you can monitor the other process, get the memory usage, window title, and importantly, pass input to the other program (if it uses 'stdin' for its input) via a 'streamwriter' and the 'StandardInput' property.

Question 63: Changing the background look of a 'TextBox' control

What should I do to use my own customized background look for a 'TextBox' control?

I don't want only to change the background color, but set some kind of input mask or have a background picture displayed. When I type in, the text will go over this customized background.

Unlike some other controls, "BackgroundImage" property is not available for 'TextBox'.

How can I do this?

A: Perhaps think about writing your own windows component that extends 'TextBox'. Start by overriding 'onPaint' and adding whatever background you want to in there.

```
protected override void OnPaint(PaintEventArgs e){
  Graphics g = e.Graphics;

  g.drawImage(myImage, 0, 0, Width, Height);
  g.drawString(Text, myFont, new SolidBrush(myColour), new
Rectangle(0, 0, Width, Height);
}
```

You're probably also going to want to draw a cursor, and perhaps one or two other things. There are methods in 'TextBox' to do this.

Note that variables starting with 'my' should be set using your gumption. Text, Width and Height are defined and controlled by inherited code.

Question 64: Replacing first line text in a "RichTextBox"

Suppose I have a 'TextBox' component and a 'RichTextBox' component on a form. When I click a button, I want the text in the 'TextBox' component to be fed into the 'RichTextBox' component first line. I'm using code as follows:

```
string str1 = textBox1.Text;
richTextBox1.Lines[0] = str1;
```

Unfortunately this code does not do the trick. The text in the 'RichTextBox' remains unchanged.

How can I pull this off ?

A: I'm not sure if you want to replace the first line or insert to the first line.

For inserting:

```
richTextBox1.Text = textBox1.Text + "\n" + richTextBox1.Text
```

For removing and replacing:

```
//Make sure to check if box is empty
richTextBox1.Text =
richTextBox1.Text.Remove(0,richTextBox1.Lines[0].Length);
richTextBox1.Text = textBox1.Text + richTextBox1.Text;
```

Question 65: Events

I know how to make use of events. I use events like 'paint' and 'onClick' all the time. But how can I create my own? I want to trigger an event whenever the rendered I'm writing has completed another object.

Is there a way for me to do this?

A: If the rendered you're working with is a user control, then making your own custom events isn't too complicated. Add a property to the form that looks like this:

```
public event EventHandler YourEventName;
```

Whenever you want that event to occur, the line:

```
YourEventName(this, new EventArgs());
```

will raise the event. One more helpful tidbit is to make a structure a raised event like so:

```
if (YourEventName != null)
   YourEventName(this, new EventArgs());
```

The reason I check for null is if I raise the event while the control is loading, an error occurs.

Question 66: DLL

How can I make a project compile into a DLL?

A: Go into your solution settings. Right-click on your 'solution', in the solution window selects "Properties". The type of project is in there. Rebuild. Fix any errors. Then, rebuild again.

Question 67: Mouse co-ords

I am trying to move a picture on a form when the mouse "drags" it. On "form.mousemove", the co-ord flowed in nicely until I am on the picture I want to move.

The picture seems to be "on top" of the form, and no 'mousemove' event was called.

Code:

```
    private void box_mousedown(object sender,
System.Windows.Forms.MouseEventArgs e)
    {
        mousedown = true;

        int MouseX = UserControl3.MousePosition.X;//X cordinate
        int MouseY = UserControl3.MousePosition.Y;//Y Cordinate
        if ((MouseX>box.Location.X) &&
(MouseX<(box.Location.X+box.Size.Width)) &&
            (MouseY>box.Location.Y) &&
(MouseY<(box.Location.Y+box.Size.Height)))
        {
            MessageBox.Show("Not In Box!");
            inboxques = false;}
        else
        {//ie in the box
            inboxques = true;
        }
        }
    }

    private void box_mouseup(object sender,
System.Windows.Forms.MouseEventArgs e)
    {
    mousedown = false;
    }

    private void m(object sender, System.EventArgs e)
    {

    }
```

```
        private void form1_mousemove(object sender,
System.Windows.Forms.MouseEventArgs e)
    {
    Console.WriteLine("Mouse move!"+tmpcount);
        tmpcount++;
        if (mousedown == true)
        {

        //MessageBox.Show("X :
"+UserControl3.MousePosition.X);
        //box.Location = new
System.Drawing.Point(UserControl3.MousePosition.X-300, 16);
        }

    }
```

What am I doing wrong?

A: It's very peculiar that you are having problems with moving the mouse. Nevertheless, there are two suggested codes that you can try.

You can try the following code:

```
Point dragFrom = new Point();

private void box_MouseDown(object sender,
System.Windows.Forms.MouseEventArgs e){
  dragFrom.X = e.X; //keep a record of where the mouse is
  dragFram.Y = e.Y; //you can use this to offset the box location
}

private void box_MouseMuve(object sender,
System.Windows.Forms.MouseEventArgs e){
  if(e.Button == MouseButtons.Left){
    box.Location.X = e.X - dragFrom.X; //I'm not 100% sure you can
access Location.X directly
    box.Location.Y = e.Y - dragFrom.Y; //if not, just alter location my
creating a new Point object
  }
}
```

You can also try the following code:

```
MouseMove += new
System.Windows.Forms.MouseEventHandler(this.extraMouseMove);

private void box_MouseMuve(object sender,
System.Windows.Forms.MouseEventArgs e){
  MessageBox.show("mouse movement recognized");
}
```

Question 68: Key check

I want to see if certain keys are pressed, so I can scroll a window if the user is holding down the space bar.

"Windows.Forms.Control" has the static property 'ModifierKeys', but that only works for SHIFT, CTRL, and ALT. I need something that works the same way for any key.

Is there an easy way to have the top level form receive all the 'KeyUp' and 'KeyDown' events when a 'child' control has focus?

A: Because of the way a keyboard works, you can't really look at a key and ask it if it is down or up, you can only listen for the presses. If you want to know what key was pressed, you can do the following:

1) Create an array of bools, large enough for each key code to be covered.

2) Initialize every element to 'false'.

3) Listen to the keyboard. When a key went down, change the appropriate element to 'true'. When a key went up, change it to 'false'. In java, you can use "KeyListener", but you should use the key up and down events in the 'windows.form' (the 'EventArgs' holds the answer to what key has been pressed).

4) To check the state of a key, take a look at your array.

Any form you can reach through a parent-to-parent path from your control form can listen for events. You just need to make sure the form that is listening has unbroken access. It means all the objects that are 'parents' of the "controlfor", and 'children' of your top level form should contain some kind of link to its appropriate 'child'.

The easiest way to do this is to use 'properties'. The detailed explanations are the following:

1) Child form: this triggers events such as 'KeyUp' and 'KeyDown'.

2) Direct parent of child: an instance of a 'child' appears in here. Make it publicly available through a property, thus:

```csharp
public Form child{ //don't write form, be more precise as to avoid
casting later.
  get{
    return myForm; //'myForm' is the control form
  }set{
    myForm = value;
  }
}
```

3) The top level object: the direct parent of child, is a child of this object. You can use the property to see your form through it, then listen for the event:

```csharp
myChild.child.KeyUp += new System.EventHandler(someMethod);
```

Question 69: Execute File from C#

I need to execute a file with parameters that will change on a daily basis and I'd like to do it via C#.

How can I go about executing a file from within C# code?

A: You can execute a file by using the 'Process' class under "System.Diagnostics". Like this:

```
System.Diagnostics.Process.Start("filename.exe");
```

Question 70: Calling public methods

I have a form and clicking a button instantiates a new class and loop through a series of files. After each file, I want to update a progress bar on my form to show how many files have been processed.

How can I do this? Can I use a public method on my form or is this just not possible?

I know that if I'm using a 'child mdi', I can use a cast to call back up to the 'parent' to get a public method. But how can I do it in this case?

A: The principle is to create a class with a reference to a object that created the class.

```
namespace Test
{
  class MyClass
  {
    //myForm holds a reference to the mainform.
    private Form myForm;

    //f is the form that's create MyClass
    public MyClass(Form f)
    {
      //myFrom gets the reference to the MainForm
      myForm = f;
    }

    public void loop()
    {
      for(int i = 0; i < 10; i++)
      {
        //And finally, you can call a public method in the MainForm.
        myForm.MyMethod();
      }
    }
  }
}
```

Question 71: Win32 API – CopyMemory

I'm currently working on a prototype upgrade of one of my employers larger systems from VB 6.0 to c#.Net. The current application runs off of a variety of 'Server' objects, but unfortunately when they were developed, the external provider made extensive use of RDS which is not supported by '.Net'. So, essentially we're looking to re-build almost everything from the ground up, starting at the first principles again.

Within the server side class libraries there are also references to several areas of the Win32 API, and I'm specific ally interested in the "CopyMemory" function.

In vb 6.0, this would be declared as:

Private Declare Sub CopyMemory Lib "kernel32" Alias "RtlMoveMemory" (pDst As Any, pSrc As Any, ByVal ByteLen As Long)

I can pretty much interpret this to c#, but I am a little uncertain as to how this function fits within '.Net'.

Is it supported by the Framework?

If it is, what data types can be used as input variables as the 'As Any' statement is not supported by '.Net'?

Is it comprehensive enough in Win32 API reference that could give me the detail I need?

A: Here is the declaration:

```
[DllImport("kernel32.Dll")]

private extern void  CopyMemory(
  System.IntPtr Destination, // pointer to address of copy destination
  System.IntPtr Source, // pointer to address of block to copy
  System.Int32  Length      // size, in bytes, of block to copy
);
```

Question 72: Building a Dynamic Code

I am from a PERL background and we were able to build a code dynamically. I was wondering if this is possible in C#. What I want to do is change the display of a form's options based on which files are present in a directory.

Specifically, I want to open a text file and make its contents displayed as a check box option. If selected, the contents of the text file will be included in a 'word.doc' of my choice.

I will not know in advance how many text files will exist. I am trying to make the application more 'user' configurable. In PERL, we use simple text files a lot and this is the reason for that choice, but a better alternative would be good.

How can I do this?

A: You probably want something like:

[] File 1
[] File 2
[] File 3

or:

[] Text from file 1 that may go
on for many lines...
[] Text from file 2 that may go
on for many lines...
[] Text from file 3 that may go
on for many lines...

If so, this can be done fairly easily, and you don't need to build any code dynamically (unless your files are code and you are using this program to 'build code dynamically').

For the first option, you can run through the list of files creating a new checkbox control each time, and add it to any area you would like. Then, when you switch folders, just get rid of them and start over (you will have kept them in an array of course).

Here's a small example on how to get all files from a directory:

```
DirectoryInfo currDir = new DirectoryInfo(path);
FileInfo[] files = currDir.GetFiles();
   //gets all the files in the directory
OR
string searchPattern = "*.txt";
FileInfo[] files = currDir.GetFile(searchPattern);
   //gets all .txt files

foreach(FileInfo file in files)
   //loops through the array of files
{
//...
}
```

You can also use the "FileInfo" class to open files for reading:

```
FileStream fs = file.OpenRead();
```

And then, use "fs.Read" for reading a number of bytes.

You can also take a look on the Microsoft developer network for some more information about the used objects above.

(http://msdn.microsoft.com/library/default.asp?url=/libr...)

Question 73: Namespace

I have the following 'namespaces' in project:

```
namespace service
{
   public class ServiceClass
   {
   }
}

namespace database
{
   public class DatabaseClass
   {
   }
   namespace service
   {
      public class DatabaseServiceClass
      {
      }
   }
}
```

I want to be able to access "ServiceClass" within "DatabaseClass". However, whenever I try to access it through the service namespace, I get an error.

Is there anyway I can access the "ServiceClass" from 'DatabaseClass'?

A: If you put this:

```
using ServiceClass = service.ServiceClass;
```

at the top of your program, you can then say:

```
ServiceClass sc = new ServiceClass()
```

inside of 'DatabaseClass'.

Question 74: WMI Management

I have .NET 2003 to develop C#. I am just starting to learn/code WMI apps.
My system cannot find "SYSTEM.MANAGEMENT".

Have I missed a trick?

A: Yes, you missed a trick, but fortunately it is a really easy one. You just need to add a 'reference' to the 'System.Management' component.

Here are the detailed directions for adding the reference you need from within the IDE:

1) Right click on "References" in the solution explorer.
2) Click on "Add Reference ..." on the popup menu.
3) Scroll down in the selection list until you get to the "System." section containing "System.Management".
4) Double click on "System.Management".
5) Click on "OK" at the bottom of the dialog box.

That's it. Now, the IDE and compiler will recognize "System.Management", and it will add the appropriate switch to the compilation so the compiler and runtime will recognize it too.

Question 75: Console application

I'd like my console application to read data from a text file which resides in the same directory as the application. Console doesn't seem to have an 'Application' class like that found in "Windows.Forms".

Is there something else I can use to determine my application's path?

A: Here are two methods:

1) "Environment.GetCommandLineArgs()" returns an array containing all of the command line arguments. The first argument in this array is the canonical path to the application. No matter how the application is started ("..\myApp", "debug\myApp", etc.), the first element in the array will have the full path to your application, including the drive letter.

E.g.

string appStartupFolder = new System.IO.FileInfo(Environment.GetCommandLineArgs()[0]).DirectoryName

2) "System.Reflection.Assembly.GetEntryAssembly()" returns the path (including the filename, as with "GetCommandLineArgs").

Question 76: Stringbuilder Flush

Is there a member that allows a string builder to be reset to ""?

A: There is a member that allows it, but what might be surprising at first is that it isn't a method, but a property.

Set "Length" to zero. Length is writeable in the 'StringBuilder' class. The internal buffer will be untouched (which is good for performance), and subsequent "Appends" will overwrite the old contents.

"StringBuilder" already m ust keep the allocated buffer length distinct from the in-use length. Making the property read/write just takes it to the next logical step. If you are repeatedly building up a "StringBuilder" to the same length and resetting it, you will find that after the first cycle there will be no addition heap allocations. Good performance is probably just what you are after (or you would have just allocated a new "StringBuilder" in your code in the first place instead of looking for a way to reset its contents).

You might be curious what happens if you set the length to a value "higher" than the original length. In that case, the additional space is filled with nulls.

Question 77: Validate date

I've seen a lot of complicated ways of finding out whether a date is valid or not. I have a text box which has no user input validation. I am trying to convert the entry entered in it into a date, in order to test whether or not the date is valid.

It seems to work so far, but I wonder if it is advisable to do it this way?

My code is as follows:

```
try
    {
        DateTime DateFrom =
Convert.ToDateTime(txtDateFrom.Text);
    }
    catch
    {
        lblLogResult.Text += "Invalid Date From";
    }
```

What am I doing wrong here?

A: I think it is the right way to do it.

You could also write a general function (which you would put in a utility class, i.e. Utils) for it like this:

```
public static bool IsDateTime(string value)
{
  try {
    Convert.ToDateTime(value);
    return true;
  }
  catch {
    return false;
  }
}
```

And then, your code would look like this:

```
if (Utils.IsDateTime(txtDateFrom.Text))
{
    DateTime DateFrom = Convert.ToDateTime(txtDateFro m.Text);
}
else
{
    lblLogResult.Text += "Invalid Date From";
}
```

Question 78: Changing the database path of crystal report

I have a problem in using crystal report. I have the code below in my form where mycrystal report viewer resides, and I want to programmatically change the location of the database in my crystal report before it loads. I find most part of this on MSDN, but I couldn't get it working.

Code:

```csharp
private void frmReport_Load(object sender, System.EventArgs e) {
    CrystalReport1 myReport = new CrystalReport1();
    TableLogOnInfo tbllogonInfo = new TableLogOnInfo();

//There is a compilation error here saying there is no overload that takes
1 arguments. But the Load() method has 3 overloads.
    myReport.Load(mdiContainer.strReportLoc);
//I try to delete the line above but I encountered a run-time error here. It
stated: "unable to find the report in the manifest resources."

    // Loop through every table in the report.
    for (int i=0; i == myReport.Database.Tables.Count - 1; i++) {
    // Set the connection information for the current table.
    tbllogonInfo.ConnectionInfo.ServerName =
MDIForm.strDBLoc;
        tbllogonInfo.ConnectionInfo.DatabaseName =
MDIForm.strDBLoc;
        tbllogonInfo.ConnectionInfo.UserID = "";
        tbllogonInfo.ConnectionInfo.Password = "";
        myReport.Database.Tables[i].ApplyLogOnInfo
(tbllogonInfo);
    }

        crystalReportViewer1.ReportSource =
mdiContainer.strReportLoc;
    }
```

What can I do to solve my problem? I'm using MS Access 2000 as my database.

A: You can use the "ReportDocument" object model (in a web app, but it shouldn't make a difference), not a strong type but works fine:

```
using CrystalDecisions.Shared;
using CrystalDecisions.CrystalReports.Engine;

///////////

private void GetReport()
{
ReportDocument oRpt = new ReportDocument();
oRpt.Load(reportPath);

TableLogOnInfo logOnInfo = new TableLogOnInfo();
ConnectionInfo connectionInfo = new ConnectionInfo();
connectionInfo = logOnInfo.ConnectionInfo;

connectionInfo.ServerName = reportServer;
connectionInfo.DatabaseName = dbName;
connectionInfo.UserID    = uId;
connectionInfo.Password = pwd;

for(int i=0;i<oRpt.Database.Tables.Count;i++)
{
oRpt.Database.Tables[i].ApplyLogOnInfo(logOnInfo);
if(!oRpt.Database.Tables[i].TestConnectivity)
{
  //process connection error
}
}

crViewer.ReportSource = oRpt;
}
```

Question 79: Calling Notepad

If in VB NET there are 'shell()' command to execute other '*.exe' in Windows system directory, and VCPP has 'Winexec()' to call other executable file.

What function in Visual C# makes equal action?

A: You can try the two examples below.

Example 1:

```
try
{
//string m_FilePathToOpen ="...";
System.Diagnostics.Process vProcess=new
System.Diagnostics.Process();
vProcess.EnableRaisingEvents =false;
vProcess.StartInfo.FileName= "notepad.exe";
//vProcess.StartInfo.Arguments= m_FilePath;
vProcess.Start();
}
catch (Exception e)
{
  //
}
```

Example 2:

```
string WorkingDirectory = "C:\\Applications";
try
{
System.Diagnostics.Process p = new System.Diagnostics.Process();
p.StartInfo.CreateNoWindow = true;
p.StartInfo.WorkingDirectory = WorkingDirectory;
p.StartInfo.FileName =  WorkingDirectory + "\\" + "my.exe";
p.StartInfo.Arguments = " ...";   // build here the
arguments
p.EnableRaisingEvents = true;      // if you want to capture events
p.StartInfo.UseShellExecute = false;
p.Exited += new EventHandler(captureOut);
```

```
p.Start();
}
catch(Exception exProcess)
{
}

private void captureOut(object sender, EventArgs e)
{
System.Diagnostics.Process ps = (System.Diagnostics.Process)
sender;
// ...
}
```

Question 80: Dynamically creating a web control

I am able to create a web control programmatically and display it on the form. In the 'click event' of the button, I am trying to capture the value entered in the created 'textbox' in another click of the button. But I am unable to obtain the reference of the control that has b een created dynamically.

```
protected System.Web.UI.WebControls.Panel myPanel;

private void btnMake_Click(object sender, System.EventArgs e)
{
    TextBox txtBox = new TextBox();
    myPanel.Controls.Add(txtBox);

}
private void btnGotValues_Click(object sender, System.EventArgs e)
{
    TextBox myTextBox =(TextBox)myPanel.Controls[1];
    lblMessage.Text = myTextBox.Text;
    lblMessage.Visible = true;
}
```

How can I make this right?

A: You need to keep loading your control once it's created. Otherwise, you'll lose a reference to it. Second, the 'Controls Collection' is zero based.

```
private void Page_Load(object sender, System.EventArgs e)
{
if(ViewState["TextBoxCreated"] != null)
{
 addTextBox();
}
}
private void addTextBox()
{
  myPanel.Controls.Clear();
  TextBox txtBox = new TextBox();
  myPanel.Controls.Add(txtBox);
```

```
}
private void btnMake_Click(object sender, System.EventArgs e)
{
addTextBox();
ViewState["TextBoxCreated"] = true;
}
private void btnGotValues_Click(object sender, System.EventArgs e)
{
TextBox myTextBox =(TextBox)PlaceHolder1.Controls[0];
lblMessage.Text = myTextBox.Text;
lblMessage.Visible = true;
}
```

Question 81: Opening Form2 from Form1

I have three menu items in 'Form1', and when I select any of them I want to open 'Form2'. However, I need to show different label captions and make some controls visible or invisible depending on the menu item I select. I think I need to pass a flag 0, 1, 2 depending on the menu selected, and then show the form depending on the flag. I am currently using this in the 'menu click event' of 'Form1' to invoke 'Form2'.

```
Form2 frm = new Form2();
frm.OnOkClickedEvent += new
Form2.OnOkClicked(HandleEventSet);
frm.ShowDialog(this);
```

This currently handles the selections made in 'Form2'.

How can I improve this?

A: The trick is to work the '.NET' way and use a custom enumeration. This makes your code much more readable.

For instance, before the declaration for your first form (you can also create all enumerators in a separate file), declare a new enumerator:

```
public enum MenuSelected
{
    None,
    ItemOne,
    ItemTwo,
    ItemThree
}
```

The next step is to make sure that all your delegates points to the same event handler. This can be done in the designer by selecting the same method for each "menuItem". Click 'event'.

However, the code is the following:

```
menuItem2.Click += new System.EventHandler(OnMenuSelect);
menuItem3.Click += new System.EventHandler(OnMenuSelect);
menuItem4.Click += new System.EventHandler(OnMenuSelect);
```

In the event method itself, you can do the following:

1. Instantiate 'Form2'.
2. Make sure that the "sender" is a menu item.
3. Find out which object actually initiated the event.
4. Run a "PrepareForm" method on 'Form2' which will do any pre-processing before.
5. Show the form.

Here is the code:

```
private void OnMenuSelect(object sender, System. EventArgs e)
{
  // Instantiate Form2
  Form2 frm2 = new Form2();
  if (sender is MenuItem)
  {
    // Cast sender to MenuItem in order to access the specific methods
    MenuItem mi = (MenuItem)sender;
    MenuSelected selectedItem = MenuSelected.None;
    // Find out which menuitem initiated the event.
    switch (mi.Text)
    {
      case "Menu Item 1":
        selectedItem = MenuSelected.ItemOne;
        break;
      case "Menu Item 2":
        selectedItem = MenuSelected.ItemTwo;
        break;
      case "Menu Item 3":
        selectedItem = MenuSelected.ItemThree;
        break;
    }
    // execute method passing our enumerator
    frm2.PrepareForm(selectedItem);
    frm2.Show();
  }
}
```

In 'Form2', all you need to implement is the "PrepareForm" method:

```csharp
public void PrepareForm(MenuSelected selectedItem)
{
    if (selectedItem == MenuSelected.ItemOne)
        MessageBox.Show("Item One Selected");
    if (selectedItem == MenuSelected.ItemTwo)
        MessageBox.Show("Item Two Selected");
    if (selectedItem == MenuSelected.ItemThree)
        MessageBox.Show("Item Three Selected");

}
```

Question 82: File read

How can I read an entirely small ASCII text file in a string variable?

A: Even there is a small file a "StringBuilder" will be used to read in the whole file.

```
using System;
using System.IO;
using System.Text;
StringBuilder ReadFile(string sPathFile)
{
    StreamReader sr = null;
    System.Text.StringBuilder sb = null;
    try
    {
        sb = new System.Text.StringBuilder();
        sr = new StreamReader(sPathFile);
        string line ="";
        while ((line = sr.ReadLine()) != null)
        {
            sb.Append (line);
        }
    }
    catch (Exception e)
    {
    string sMsg = "Error reading file : " + sPathFile + " into a
StringBuilder " + e.GetType() + e.Message;
    throw new Exception (sMsg);
    }
        finnaly
        {
        if (sr !=null)
        sr.Close();
        sr = null;
        }
    return sb;
}
```

How to use:

```
StringBuilder sb = ReadFile("C:\\todo.txt");
if (sb !=null)
{
 string sTemp = sb.ToString();
}
```

Question 83: Close-open

I have a timer in one of my forms (frmFlash), which after 2 seconds should close the form and open another (frmMain). The problem is, after the timer closes 'frmFlash', 'frmMain' does not open.

But if I display a message box during 'frmMain's' Load procedure, there is no problem and the form (frmmain) I want to show opens.

How can I correct this?

A: I'm not sure at what moment you're trying to run this, but the controlling program needs to be in the same scope.

For instance:

If you were trying to display a 'splash screen', you would write the following:

```
[STAThread]
static void Main()
{
    Form1 frm = new Form1();
    frm.ShowDialog();
    Application.Run(new Form2());
}
```

Execution of this code will now halt until 'Form1' is closed.

The timer is in 'Form1'. On the 'Tick' event, you would call this event method:

```
private void timer1_Elapsed(object sender,
System.Timers.ElapsedEventArgs e)
{
    this.Close();
}
```

It will close 'Form1' and allow the "Application.Run" to execute.

If you were not doing this is the start-up, just omit the "Application.Run" and instantiate the 'Form2', and call the ".Show method".

Question 84: Using "foreach" to enumerate objects

I want to find a way to enumerate my objects (such as textboxes, buttons, etc) in my form using 'foreach' statement. I don't know how to do this in C#.

Is there an instruction on how to do this?

A: You can try the following:

```
System.Windows.Forms.Form frm = new
System.Windows.Forms.Form ();
//... Add controls in the frm
// Enumerate the controls

foreach (Control ctrl in frm.Controls)
{
    // ... ctrl
    Type t = ctrl.GetType();
    // ...
}
```

This can be done to any object that implements the 'IEnumerable' interface. If you look in the 'help', you'll find a list of objects on which you can do "foreach(){}". It goes from 'Array' to 'XmlSchemaCollection'.

You can implement this interface in your classes too:

```
using System.Collections;
using System.Drawing;

class Triangle : IEnumerable
{
    public Point A, B, C;

    // declare method required by IEnumerable
    public IEnumberator GetEnumerator()
    {
        return new PointEnumerator(this);
    }
```

```csharp
// Inner class implements IEnumerator interface
private class PointEnumerator : IEnumerator
{
  private int position = -1;
  private Triangle t;

  // constructor
  public PointEnumerator(Triangle t)
  {
    this.t = t;  // make a local copy of the Triangle object
  }

  // Declare the public method required by IEnumerator
  public bool MoveNext()
  {
    if (position < (3 - 1) // three points in triangle,
                   // subtract one for starting at 0
      position++;
      return true;
    }
    else
    {
      return false;
    }
  }

  // declare the public method required by IEnumerator
  public void Reset()
  {
    position = -1;
  }

  // declare the public property required by IEnumerator
  public object Current
  {
    get
    {
      switch (position)
      {
        case 0:
          return t.A.ToObject();
          break;
        case 1:
```

```
            return t.B.ToObject();
            break;
        case 2:
            return t.C.ToObject();
            break;
        default:
            return null;
            break;
        }
      }
    }
  }
}
```

What this code does is declare a class named 'Triangle' that implements the "IEnumerable" interface. It will allow you to go through the points of the triangle using the "foreach(){}" operator.

"IEnumerable" uses another interface named "IEnumerator", which does all the dirty work. It requires you to implement two methods and a property. The methods reset the position to the beginning, and move the position to the next point. The property retrieves whatever 'Point' is current.

This is actually a good example for someone new to C# and '.NET', as it illustrates some cool features of the language: private classes (classes which are only visible inside their containing class), interfaces (programming by contract, always write a code which will implement the interface), and passing a reference to an object to another object via its constructor method.

Some notes on doing this:

The Point object is a value type, not a reference type (meaning it's a structure, not a class). When the 'Current' property returns one, it has to call "ToObject" (since 'Current' demands it to be an object). This involves what's known as "boxing" the 'Point' object, which is converting the value type to a reference type. This is inherently slow, as the calling function would have to cast it (it's now an Object) back into a 'Point' data type before accessing the '.x' and '.y' properties of a 'Point'. Which brings up another point (pun intended), "IEnumerator" only knows about 'Objects'. This means you could cast into another data type other than a 'Point'. When the next version of '.NET' comes out, you will be able to use 'Generics', which prevents this feature/problem.

Question 85: Connection to MS SQL

I'm using C# and trying to connect to one data base which is on the same computer with IIS.

Here is mistake message:

"SELECT permission denied on object 'tblUsers', database 'banking', owner 'dbo'.
Description: An unhandled exception occurred during the execution of the current web request. Please review the stack trace for more information about the error and where it originated in the code."

Exception Details: System.Data.SqlClient.SqlException: SELECT permission denied on object 'tblUsers', database 'banking', owner 'dbo'.

Source Error:

```
Line 29:      private void Page_Load(object sender,
System.EventArgs e)
Line 30:      {
Line 31:        sqlDataAdapter1.Fill(DataSet1);
Line 32:        DataGrid1.DataBind();
Line 33:      }
```

What doest it mean? How can I fight this problem?

A: Not to be obvious, but it means that you don't have select permission on the table you're trying to select from as the user you're connecting to SQL Server with.

You can check permissions on the table with 'enterprise manager'. Select the table, then "Action->All Tasks->Manager Permissions". You'll probably find that nothing is checked for public (anyone) or the user you're connecting as.

Question 86: Hard returns in a string replace assistance

I'm using C# for a code behind in an 'ASP.NET' site.

Users are entering information into a database and later display same. Some entries have hard returns in them. When it's redisplayed, the hard returns are not recognized and the formatting was wrong.

I need a way to replace the hard returns at display time with <br>.

I have tried the following:

```
DisplayString.Replace(char(13), "<br>")
DisplayString.Replace("\r\n", "<br>")
```

Is there any way to use the Default "String.Replace", instead of having to dive into 'regex parsing'?

A: I believe that should work, but you need to assign the result:

```
DisplayString = DisplayString.Replace("\r\n", "<br>")
```

Question 87: ArrayList

Can any one tell me how to do the following? At the moment, I created a new array list.

ArrayList Code = new ArrayList()

I then pass this to a class function which will load the array with a field from a table. Then, on the return from loading the assigned array to a combo box:

cbCatCode.DataSource = Code;

These all works but I would like to load the array with (say) two fields and not just one.

Then I assigned just one on the array items to the combo box. So, the array has:

code name
code name
code name

and so on. I just want the code part to display in the combo.

Can this be done?

A: There's no certainty if an 'ArrayList' can have multi-dimensions. Maybe you can try that?

ArrayList Code = new ArrayList();
--load with data--

ArrayList Name = new ArrayList();
--load--

ArrayList CodeANDName = new ArrayList(2);
CodeANDName.Add(Code);
CodeANDName.Add(Name);

Question 88: Standard text box

I'm trying to capture the data in a standard text box (usually a numeric part number. IE: '57231'), and use it to search a specific location on a network server for an image with the same number. The number is always the same name as the image file which is appended with a '.JPG' extension.

How can I write the code to append the ".jpg" extension and point to the network share where the pictures are, so that the application can find the correct photo and display it in my picture box?

A: You can try the following:

```
string str1 = "First string, ";
string str2 = "Second string";
string str3 = str1 + str2;
Console.WriteLine(str3);
```

This will output: First string, Second string.

In your case, suppose the textbox were called 'txtBox1', it can be something like this:

```
string filename = txtBox1.Text + ".jpg";
```

That will give you the file name you're looking for. The rest should be fairly straight forward.

```
string str1 = "First string, ";
string str2 = "Second string";
string str3 = str1 + str2;
Console.WriteLine(str3);
```

A better approach is to use the 'Path' class from "System.IO" namespace. It will handle any backslashes, etc. that may be necessary.

```
string pathpart1 = "c:\\MyFiles";
string pathpart2 = txtBox1.Text;
```

```
string pathextension = ".jpg";

string fullpath = Path.Combine(Path.Combine(pathpart1,
            pathpart2), pathextension);
```

I'm not sure, but I believe it will also work with a UNC path.

If you want to get the best response to a question, please check out "FAQ222-2244" first.

You can also use this snippet:

```
//create variable for Image file "ImgFile" which is pulled from the Part
No. Field in the form.

string ImgFile = "";

if (txtVenCode.Text == "")
  {
    MessageBox.Show("You must enter a Vendor Code and   Part
Number to perform a search.");
  }
else if (txtPartNo.Text == "")
  {
    MessageBox.Show("You must enter a Vendor Code and Part
Number to perform a search.");
  }
else
  {
    ImgFile = @"Y:\WebCatalog\images\parts\" + txtPartNo.Text+
".jpg";
      if (!System.IO.File.Exists(ImgFile))
      {
      MessageBox.Show("The file does not exist");
      }
    else
      {
      pbxPartImg.Image = Image.FromFile   (ImgFile);
      }
  }
```

Question 89: Error when trying to run a file

I am trying to launch a file as follows:

```
Process proc = new Process();
proc.StartInfo.RedirectStandardError=true;
proc.StartInfo.RedirectStandardInput=false;
proc.StartInfo.RedirectStandardOutput=false;
proc.StartInfo.CreateNoWindow=true;
proc.StartInfo.ErrorDialog=false;
proc.StartInfo.UseShellExecute=false;
proc.StartInfo.FileName = @"C:\ftpFeed\ftpFeedGen
/Url:http://testmachine/webpath/engine.asmx/getFile?CompanyKey=D
emoTest /File:file03022004_051011.xml /User: ftp /pwd: password";
proc.Start();
```

It is giving me the following error:

"The filename, directory name, or volume label syntax is incorrect."

If I copy and paste my file into a command window, it runs fine.

Is there a correction for this?

A: I think what you want is:

```
proc.StartInfo.FileName = @"C:\ftpFeed\ftpFeedGen";
proc.StartInfo.Arguments =
"/Url:http://testmachine/webpath/engine.asmx/getFile?CompanyKey=D
emoTest /File:file03022004_051011.xml /User: ftp /pwd: password";
```

Question 90: Basic Treeview

How do I do the following in a C# within a 'Treeview' in C# code?

```
Root
 Parent1
   Child1
   Child2
 Parent2
   Child1
   Child3
```

A: You can try the following example:

```
TreeNode root = new TreeNode("Root");
tv.Nodes.Add(root);

TreeNode parent = new TreeNode("Parent1");
root.Nodes.Add(parent);

parent.Nodes.Add(new TreeNode("Child1"));
parent.Nodes.Add(new TreeNode("Child 2"));

parent = new TreeNode("Parent2");
root.Nodes.Add(parent);

parent.Nodes.Add(new TreeNode("Child1"));
parent.Nodes.Add(new TreeNode("Child3"));
```

VBXL

Question 91: Update an XML file in C#

I'm trying to update an XML file from C#.

I have the following 'filePath' as a string:

```
<Model>
    <Locations>
        <BenefitsLocation>
        <Name>Benfits Location</Name>
        <FilePath>"C:\\WhereEver"</FilePath>
        </BenefitsLocation>
    </Locations>
</Model>
```

How would I go about updating this?

A: There are many solutions to that:

1.
- Load the xml file into an 'XmlDocument'.
- Locate the element that you want to update.
- Update it (in memory) if found.
- Save the 'XmlDocument' into the same xml file.

2.
-Load the xml file into a 'DataSet' object (one line of code).
-Locate there the elements to be updated.
-Update the elements.
-Save the 'DataSet' object into the xml file (one line of code).

3. ///

Example :

```
bool bModified = false;
XmlDocument oXmlDocument = new XmlDocument();
oXmlDocument.Load("myfile.xml");
const string filePath = "Model/Locations/BenefitsLocation/FilePath";
XmlNode n =oXmlDocument.SelectSingleNode(filePath))
if (n != null)
{
```

```
     n.InnerText = "new path";
     bModified = true;

}
if (bModified)
   oXmlDocument.Save("myfile.xml");
```

You can write a function which takes a parameter on the node name you want to set, and the new value to put there.

This function locates the node which you want to change the value, and set the 'InnerText' property to that value and calls "Save()".

```
void UpdateSettings(string key, string val)
{
try
{
   XmlDocument oXmlDocument = new XmlDocument();
   oXmlDocument.Load("settings.xml");
   System.Xml.XmlNode n = oXmlDocument.SelectSingleNode(key);
   if (n!=null)
   {
     n.InnerText= val;
   }
   //
   oXmlDocument.Save("settings.xml");

}catch()
  {
  }
}
UpdateSettings("//router//name",myForm.nameTextBox1.Text);
```

It's the same, but then as a function it takes a string from a form.

Question 92: Print an image

How can I print a picture like a 'jpg' or 'gif' in C#?

A: There are "PrintDocument" and "Graphics" classes.

Here is a small example:

```
private void printButton_Click(object sender, EventArgs e)
{
  try
  {
    // Assumes the default printer.
    PrintDocument pd = new PrintDocument();
    pd.PrintPage += new PrintPageEventHandler(this.pd_PrintPage);
    pd.Print();
  }
  catch(Exception e)
  {
    MessageBox.Show("Error occurred while printing", e.GetType() +
e.Message);
  }
}

private void pd_PrintPage(object sender, PrintPageEventArgs ev)
{
  // Draw image.
  ev.Graphics.DrawImage(Image.FromFile("C:\\Program
Files\\Images\\george.bmp"), ev.Graphics.VisibleClipBounds);
  // Indicate that this is the last page to print.
  ev.HasMorePages = false;
}
```

Question 93: ListBox and Access

'ListBox' can bind 'dataset' right?

I have an Access database (say I have 'a.mdb' and it has 1 table (XY table), and 2 fields 'x' and 'y'). I can connect it with my app using "OleDBconnection" and manipulating using "oleDBcommand".

My questions are:

1. I want to access x field (in xy table), and every data in the x field becomes a list of item in a 'listBox1'. How can I do that?

2. The changes in a 'listbox1' were reflected in my database too. I mean if I delete an item using "removeat", so in the database that selected row is deleted too.

How can I do that?

A: For the first question, you can try the following:

```
foreach(DataRow dataRow in dataTable.Rows)
{
   comboBox1.Items.Add(dataRow"x");
}
```

For the second question, you can try the following:

Within the event, that removes the item. You could manually remove it from the DB.

Set up the "DataAdapter's DeleteCommand" property to:

"DELETE * FROM _Table_ WHERE _FieldName_ = _UID_;"

UID is the primary key's value for the row that you want to delete. How you get that from the information in the 'listbox' depends on how you've set things up.

Then, open the 'dataconnection' object, run:

Adapter.DeleteCommand.ExecuteNonQuery();

and 'Close' the 'dataconnection'.

Question 94: No read access for mdb using OleDbConnection

I am trying to read out some tables of a regular XP access MDB, but I keep getting an error message that I have no read privileges.

```
string strDSN = "Provider=Microsoft.Jet.OLEDB.4.0; Data Source=" +
strDatabaseFile;
string strSQL = "SELECT Name FROM MSysObjects WHERE Type
= 1;";
OleDbConnection myConn = new OleDbConnection(strDSN);
OleDbCommand myCmd = new OleDbCommand( strSQL, myConn );
OleDbDataReader datareader = null;
try
{
   myConn.Open();
   datareader =
myCmd.ExecuteReader(CommandBehavior.CloseConnection);
   while (datareader.Read() )
   {
      string strTest = (string) datareader"Name";
      MessageBox.Show(strTest,"hi", MessageBoxButtons.OK,
MessageBoxIcon.Exclamation);
   }
}
catch (Exception ee)
{
   MessageBox.Show("Sorry, I was not able to read from " +
strDatabaseFile + ":\n\n" + ee.Message, "An error occurred",
MessageBoxButtons.OK, MessageBoxIcon.Exclamation);
}
finally
{
   myConn.Close();
}
```

Am I missing something here?

The access on a regular table worked, but not on the 'MSys-table'.

How can this be done?

A: In Access 9X version, you would go to:

1. Tools -> Security -> User and Group Permissions;
2. Select object type "Tables" (combo box);
3. Scroll the window (Object Name) above, and select 'MSysObjects' or any other table you need to access;
4. Check the read data box;
5. Click 'OK';

Question 95: Making a button default in web forms

How can I make a button as an "AcceptButton" on a web page? (that is when I press 'enter', this button click to action should happen)

A: Buttons can act in two ways. You can have a 'Submit' button, where your ".aspx" looks like this:

```
<asp:Button id="SubmitButton"
    Text="Submit"
    OnClick="SubmitBtn_Click"
    runat="server"/>
```

This is the default, and acts like a traditional HTML button. You can also have 'Command' buttons, which appears in your 'code-behind' page as 'command events':

```
asp:Button id="SortAscendingButton"
    Text="Sort Ascending"
    CommandName="Sort"
    CommandArgument="Ascending"
    OnCommand="CommandBtn_Click"
    runat="server"/>
```

This is useful when you have multiple buttons that can submit a page, as your 'code-behind' then has a 'select-case' structure to determine which button was clicked.

Question 96: Browse Button

Is there an easy (built-in) way to make a browse button, which opens up a browse window and returns the 'pathname' to a file?

A: You can try the following:

Code:

```
OpenFileDialog ofdMyDialog = new OpenFileDialog();

ofdMyDialog.Filter = "Text Files (*.txt)|*.txt|All Files (*.*)|*.*";
ofdMyDialog.CheckFileExists = true;

string strFileName = string.empty;
if (ofdMyDialog.ShowDialog() == DialogResult.OK)
{
// They clicked the ok button, should have a pathname here
strFileName = ofdMyDialog.FileName;
}
```

Question 97: Event handler for link button in data grid

This is my data grid:

```
<asp:datagrid id="dgCities" style="Z-INDEX: 220; LEFT: 266px;
POSITION: absolute; TOP: 512px" runat="server" Width="200px"
BorderWidth="0px" CellPadding="2" CellSpacing="1" PagerStyle-
Mode="NumericPages" AllowPaging="True"
AutoGenerateColumns="False">
        <AlternatingItemStyle Font-Size="Smaller" Font-
Names="Arial" HorizontalAlign="Left" ForeColor="#9B6967"
BackColor="#DEB8B3"></AlternatingItemStyle>
        <ItemStyle Font-Size="Smaller" Font-Names="Arial"
HorizontalAlign="Left" ForeColor="#9B6967"
BackColor="#F1E3DF"></ItemStyle>
        <HeaderStyle Font-Size="Smaller" Font-Names="Arial"
Font-Bold="True" HorizontalAlign="Left" ForeColor="#F1E3DF"
BackColor="#9B6967"></HeaderStyle>
        <Columns>
            <asp:TemplateColumn HeaderText="City">
              <ItemTemplate>
                <asp:LinkButton Runat="server" text='<%#
DataBinder.Eval(Container.DataItem, "City") %>'
OnClick="Show_city">
                </asp:LinkButton>
              </ItemTemplate>
            </asp:TemplateColumn>
            <asp:TemplateColumn HeaderText="Sides">
              <ItemTemplate>
                <asp:Label Runat="server" text='<%#
DataBinder.Eval(Container.DataItem, "Sides") %>'>
                </asp:Label>
              </ItemTemplate>
            </asp:TemplateColumn>
        </Columns>
        <PagerStyle Visible="False" NextPageText="" Font-
Size="Smaller" Font-Names="Arial" PrevPageText=""
HorizontalAlign="Center" ForeColor="#F1E3DF"
BackColor="#9B6967" Mode="NumericPages"></PagerStyle>
    </asp:datagrid>
```

I have a function "Show_city". In 'aspx.cs' file, I wrote its handler:

```
public void Show_city(object sender, System.EventArgs e)
    {
        Response.Write(sender.text);
    }
```

It is wrong and shows a mistake. I want to write a text property of some 'link button' in data grid. This data grid gets its information from DB.

Where did I made a mistake and how can I solve it?

A: You should cast the sender object:

```
public void Show_city(object sender, System.EventArgs e)
    {
        Response.Write((LinkButton)sender.text);
    }
```

You only need a small syntax correction:

Code:

```
public void Show_city(object sender, System.EventArgs e)
{
  Response.Write(((LinkButton)sender).Text);
}
```

Question 98: Getting a list of class/object properties

I'm looking for a sort of collection "object.properties[index].count" etc. I mean a list of the actual properties ("field names"), not any values they might contain.

Is there a way to get a list of all properties a class or an object has during runtime?

A: Use the "GetType()" method in your class, which returns you an object of type (every object inherits this from the ultimate base class, the Object class).

You can then call "GetProperties()", "GetMethods()", etc. to return you an **array** of objects.

For example:

Code:

```
Type myType = YourClassInstance.GetType();

MethodInfo[] myMethods =
myType.GetMethods(BindingFlags.Public);

for (int i = 0; i < myMethods.Length; i++)
{
    MethodInfo mi = (MethodInfo)myMethods[i];
    Console.WriteLine("MethodName is: {0}", mi.Name;
}
```

This technique is called 'Reflection', and is a very powerful part of the '.NET' framework. It's how the IDE is able to display variable contents, etc. for you in the inspector windows.

You can also find "GetProperties()" which seems to get a little closer to the actual properties only.

Question 99: Large text file: Read and Write performance problems

I'm creating an app that can do the following:

1. Reads from a text file (fixed length) using 'StreamReader'.
2. Parses each line returned (I have tried both regular expressions and just plain SubString) to obtain Forename, Surname, HouseNumber, Street, etc. for the record.
3. Makes a call to a web service to get 250 values for the record (and populates structures with these values).
4. Creates a string, which consists of:
   - the original fixed length record;
   - the 250 values, separated by commas;
5. Writes a record with the string from (4) above to a new text file, via 'StreamWriter' (so we end up with a comma delimited file).

The problem is that my 400 record text file takes 15 minutes to run (substrings versus regular expressions don't appear to be making much difference), and I am eventually going to have to process text files with 800,000 rows.

I have no control over how long the web service call will take, but I'm running out of ideas on how to speed up the file reading/writing. I have googled quite extensively but have so far not managed to get any useful hits.

The fixed-length record being parsed is about 850 characters long (and is split into 32 fields).

How can I speed things up?

A: If the program takes 15 minutes while parsing 400 records, it indicates a big problem in the parsing procedure. There are many solutions thinking of an input file with 800,000 records (e.g. a long run).

Here is easy one by 'decoupling' the reading/parsing from the web access, and writing and using intermediate files:

-input.dat = input file;
-parse.dat = parsed data required to be passed to webservice or to be sent to output;
-parse.ctl = control file that stores the index of the last record parsed, or its index followed by the last record read from the 'input.dat';
If the 'parse.ctl' record contains only the index, which means that record was successfully parsed by a previous run. The run must continue with that index + 1 record from the input file. If the record stored in 'parse.ctl' contains the index followed by information that means 'abend' happened in the previous run while parsing that record. The process should start the parsing with that record by skipping the previous records.

-result.dat=output file with data gathered by webservice and other input information;
-result.ctl= control file that stores the index of the last record processed by the webservice, or the index followed by last record passed to the webservice;

The same rule applies to the 'result.ctl' file in order to detect the last record passed to the web service, and to know from where to continue.

One part of the program will be responsible for:
-look for 'parse.ctl' file. If it is not there, create it and store "0=" there;
-read the 'parse.ctl' record. If there is only a counter stored there, that means the previous run was done with the record counted there and will continue by reading the 'input.dat' file skipping that number of records;

If the 'parse.ctl' record contains an index and record information, then that was the last record read from the input and did not parsed successfully for some reasons and not saved to 'parse.dat'. In this case, skip records from the input file and position on the record with that counter. Check eventually if they are identical, just in case when the input file was altered. If it is the first run on this input file, the 'parse.ctl' record is "0=". If it is a re-run after an 'abend', the 'parse.ctl' record looks like one of the following:

"459=" or "459=FirstName Last Name etc"

Once positioned on the right record, do the following:
- Read it and send its counter and the record information to the 'parse.ctl' file "counter=input fileds";
- Parse the record;
- Rewrite the 'parse.ctl' and store there "counter=" only.

Another thread will be started at the same time and it will do:
-look for the 'result.ctl' file. If it is not there, create it and store "o=" there;
-read 'result.ctl' file. If there is only a counter stored there, which means the previous run was done with the record counted there.

It will continue by reading the 'parse.dat' file skipping that number of records. If the 'result.ctl' contains an index and record information, then that was the last record passed to the web service. But for some reasons, it did not complete to query information and to save it to 'result.dat'.

If it is the first run on this input file, the 'result.ctl' record is "o=". If it is a re-run after an 'abend', the 'result.ctl' record looks like one of the following:

"899=" or "899=FirstName Last Name etc".

Once positioned on the right record, this thread will do:
-read record and sent its counter followed by record info to 'result.ctl';
-pass record data to the web methods;
-build the output record and save it to 'result.dat';
-rewrite the 'result.ctl' file by sending there only the record counter "counter=";

This thread terminates when there are no records in the 'parse.dat' file, or the application is interrupted. The previous one can finish before. When all is working fine, delete the 'parse.ctl' and 'result.ctl' files.

With this solution, you can see the main program will start two threads. One is to read the input file and write to 'parse.dat' file. The other one is to read the 'parse.dat' call web methods and write to 'result.dat'.

To achieve for the both threads to share the 'parse.dat' file, one read/write and another one only read. If it is a long run, you need a way to persist processed data. This solution is using regular files, but there are other solutions (Queue, MSQueue, Pipes etc).

Question 100: Simple Program with Object Reference Required Error

Here is a simple program that I wrote, but I keep getting:

"An object reference is required for the nonstatic field, method, or property 'GetRadarFiles.GetFiles.DL(string,string)'";

Code:

```
using System;
using System.Data;
using System.Net;
using System.IO;

namespace GetRadarFiles
{

    class GetFiles
    {

        static void Main(string[] args)
        {
            string sTXTURL =
"http://www.crh.noaa.gov/radar/images/DS.p20-
r/SI.karx/dd.20050414_dt.041200.gif";
            string sGIFFile = "test.gif";

            DL(sTXTURL,sGIFFile);

        }

        private void DL(string sDLURL, string sFileName)
        {
            WebClient myWebClient = new WebClient();
            myWebClient.DownloadFile(sDLURL,sFileName);

        }
    }
}
```

What can be the solution for this?

A: That will work. You need to change your method to static. You can try the following:

Code:

```
private static void DL(string sDLURL, string sFileName)
```

Index

Lightning Source UK Ltd.
Milton Keynes UK
08 February 2010

149762UK00001B/121/A